AF469257

OBSERVATIONS IN AN OCCUPIED WILDERNESS

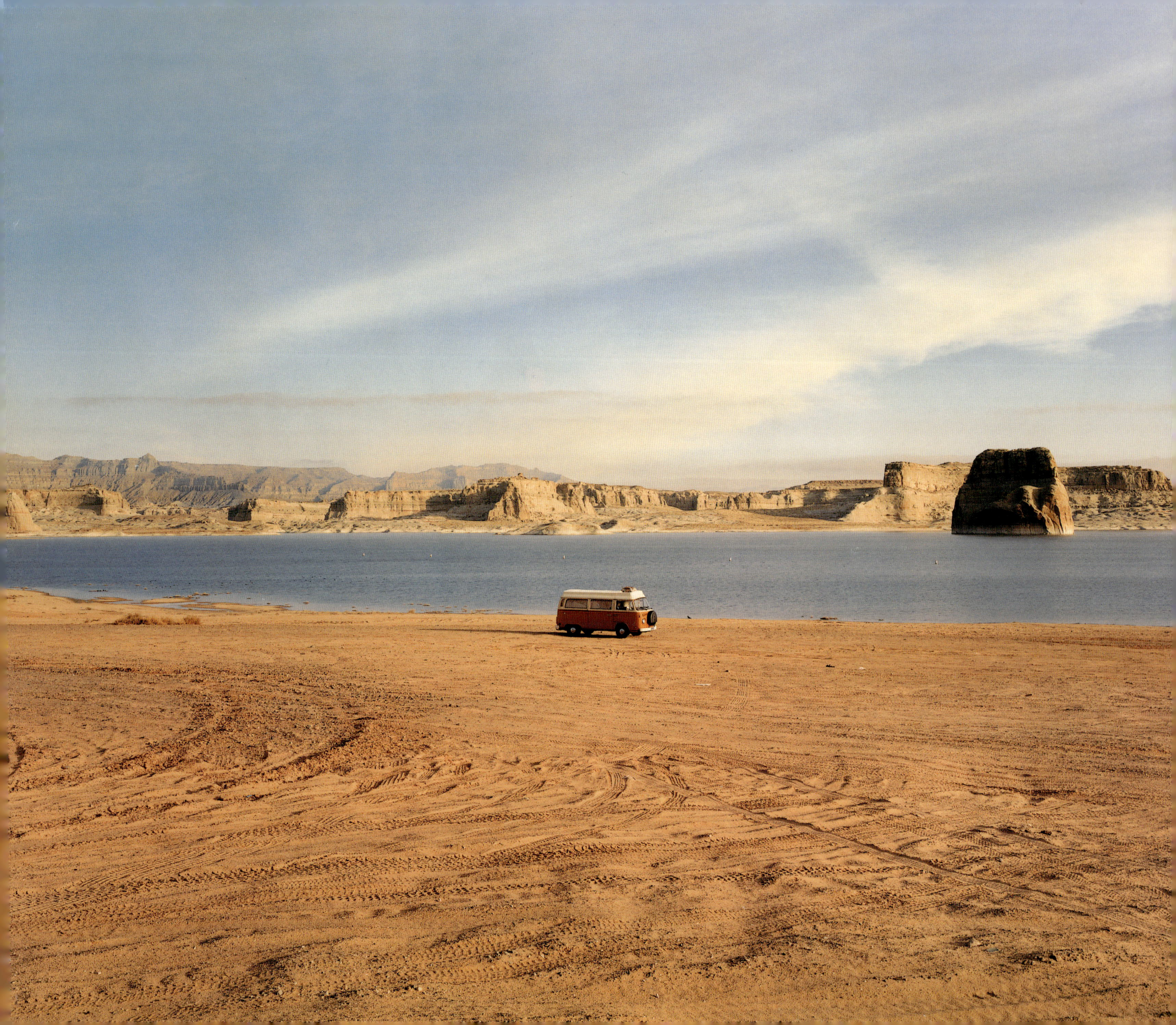

PHOTOGRAPHS BY TERRY FALKE

OBSERVATIONS IN AN OCCUPIED WILDERNESS

INTRODUCTION BY CAROL McCUSKER

ESSAY BY WILLIAM L. FOX

CHRONICLE BOOKS
SAN FRANCISCO

Library of Congress Cataloging-in-Publication Data available.

ISBN-10: 0-8118-5098-6
ISBN-13: 978-0-8118-5098-8

Manufactured in China.

Designed by **Brooke Johnson**

Distributed in Canada by Raincoast Books
9050 Shaughnessy Street
Vancouver, British Columbia V6P 6E5

10 9 8 7 6 5 4 3 2 1

Chronicle Books LLC
85 Second Street
San Francisco, California 94105

www.chroniclebooks.com

page 2: 1 | **Lake Powell,** Utah, 1997
page 120: 72 | **Leaving Navajoland,** Arizona, 1997

For my mother and father

A frog and a scorpion met at the bank of a stream. The scorpion, unable to swim, begged the frog to take him across on his back. "How do I know you won't sting me?" asked the frog. "But why would I?" said the scorpion. "We'd both drown!" The frog agreed, but as they were crossing the stream, he suddenly felt the pain of the scorpion's sting. "Why did you do that?" asked the frog. "Now you'll die, too!" Resigned to his fate, the scorpion replied, "I couldn't help it . . . it's my nature." | ATTRIBUTED TO AESOP

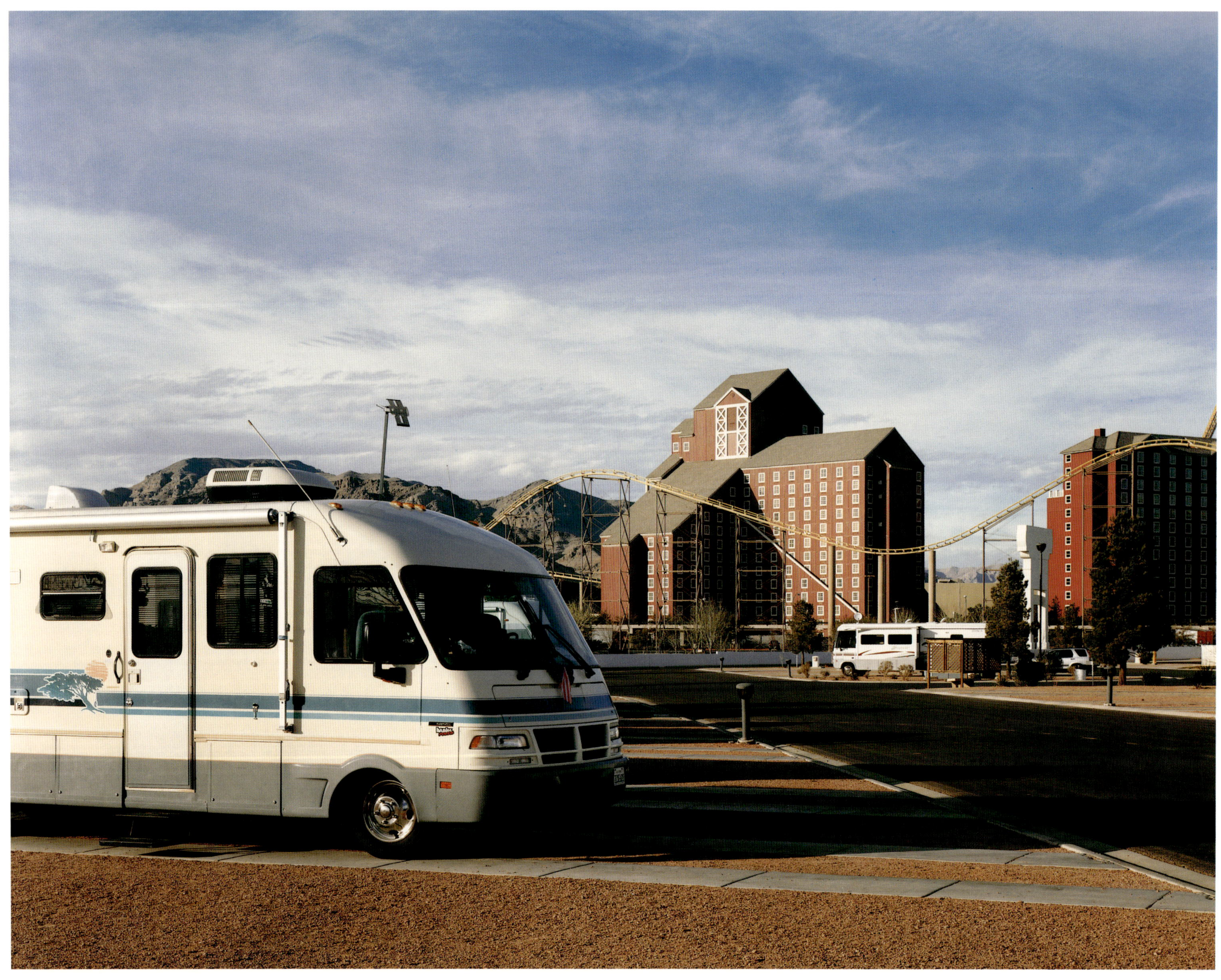

2 | **Old West–Themed Resort with Roller Coaster,** Primm, Nevada, 2001

BY CAROL McCUSKER

OBSERVING TERRY FALKE

I have driven the two-lane blacktops seen in Terry Falke's images of Kelso, the San Agustin Plains, and the Salton Sea. The urge to take to the open road may be the same for all of us: externally, to slow down to reengage the art of small observation regarding nature, time, and light. Internally, it may be to satisfy a need for solitude or a rebel instinct for self-reliance far from polite society. Over the last few decades, Falke (a veteran traveler of America's West) has noticed the presence of other sensibilities not so susceptible to the need for silence or small gestures. This book is a testimony to what he has seen.

Terry Falke was born and raised in America's Southwest. In his own words, his photographs are "personal documentary." They follow the path of his own desires and dis-ease fed by his own observations and those of fellow landscape writers and poets whom he reads regularly, Wallace Stegner, J. B. Jackson, Edward Abbey, John McPhee, Rebecca Solnit, and Yi-Fu Tuan.

He is part of a long line of photographers dedicated to observing America's West that began, more or less, with Timothy O'Sullivan. Following the Civil War, O'Sullivan's charge was to make the West visible to the politicians and industrialists back in Washington at the height of the Industrial Revolution. Almost a hundred years later, in the post–World War II era, Ansel Adams was among the last to photograph the West with O'Sullivan's optimistic eye. Adams was deeply concerned about the environment; to help us share in his concern, he foregrounded the beauty and richness of America's natural wealth. His modernist views fed the responses of politicians and conservationists alike. For the former, they pointed to an indomitable national spirit and sense of unlimited supply. For the latter, they were reminders of what greed could potentially destroy.

After Ansel Adams, the lineage fell to another Adams—Robert—but the line shifted aesthetically and politically. Falke, and the generation he runs with, are part of a postmodernist landscape movement initiated by Robert Adams. Theirs is an all-inclusive view of the landscape that does not flinch from environmental follies. Having cut their teeth on the civil rights movement and the Vietnam War, Robert Adams, Terry Falke, Richard Misrach, and Mark Klett took up the environmental banner without softening the blow. Yet Falke is also in step with Joel Sternfeld and Stephen Shore, whose less-critical view of the land advocates the sheer pleasure of *looking*.

Inevitably, or intentionally, their collective visions replaced the pastoral with a more complicated, even dystopian eye that, nonetheless, possesses its own kind of splendor. Observe Falke's photographs; in them is a love of beauty (soft light, sweeping vistas) alongside amusement or incredulity toward an ever-changing or shrinking wilderness—recreational vehicles at Sand Mountain or rockets at Lucerne Dry Lake spin into the desert's soft summer light. Telephone poles run deep into the Yuha Desert's majestic valley; century-old buildings in Valentine, Texas, and Kelso, California, list like ships in a sea of weeds. Like Roland Barthes' scrutiny of photographs in *Camera Lucida,* Falke makes me want to know: *Who lived out here? What were their daily routines? Were they content?*

One is also awed, as undoubtedly Falke is, by some of the formidable man-made structures he photographs: Parker Dam's exquisite art deco lines, Hoover Dam at dusk, the VLA (Very Large Array) out on the clear San Agustin Plains. Most of these structures were meant to be beneficial: tourist "wilderness" areas are asphalted; handrails zigzag precariously down a canyon wall. Regardless of inhospitable climes, life persists and insists: a homeless man's shopping cart in Bagdad, California, bulges with basic necessities; birds nest in a lone tree marooned in a stagnant sea; the desert pulsates with a seemingly endless supply of power lines and water conveyances.

Falke's images embody first and foremost the joy of looking at and being in the grand landscapes of the West. For the viewer concerned with such issues as drilling in the Arctic or ameliorating climate change, however, Falke's gaze is not carefree. His photographs evince an America that may be a paradise lost. . . and they beckon me to take another road trip while there is still wilderness to see.

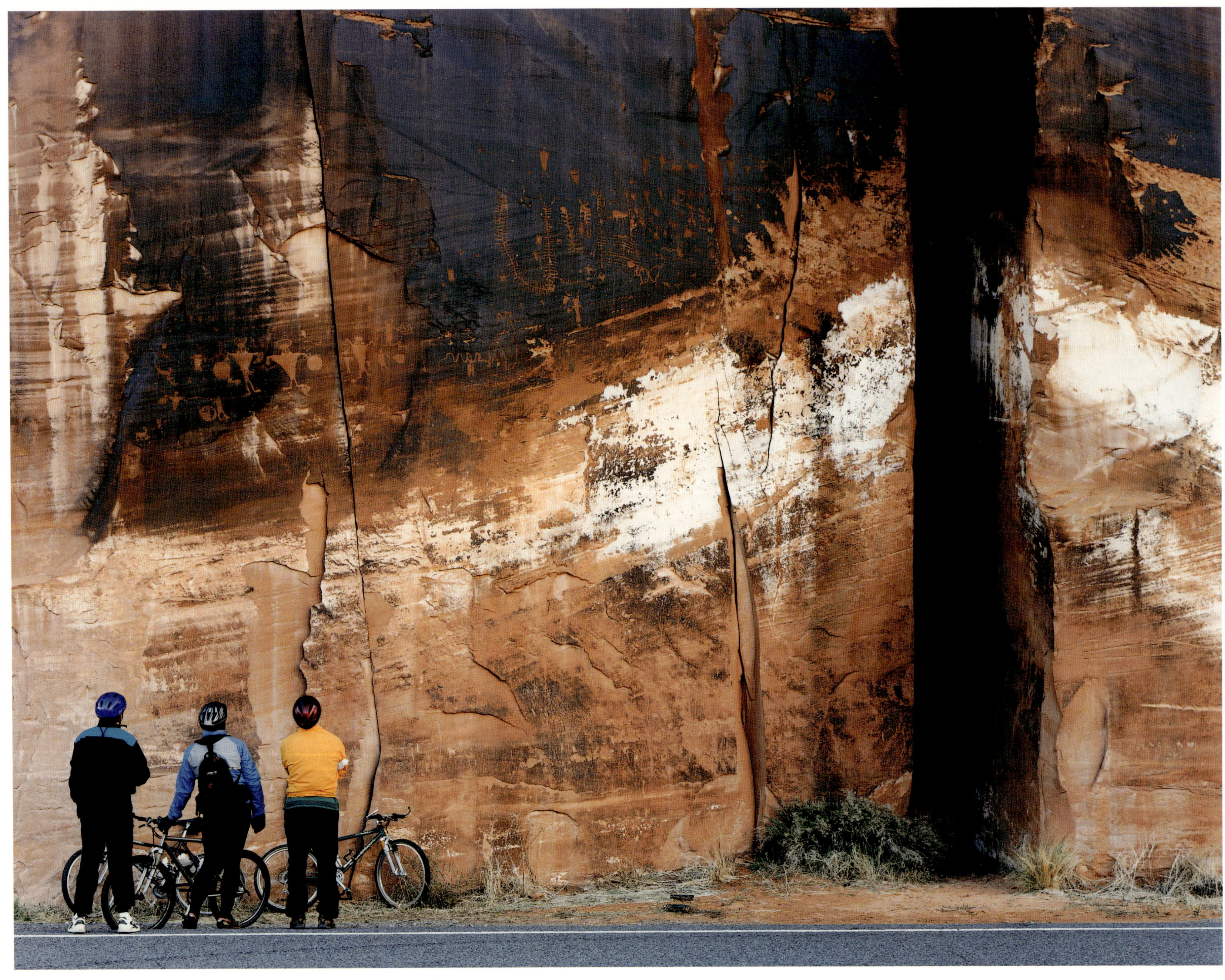

3 | **Cyclists Inspecting Ancient Petroglyphs,** Utah, 1998

BY WILLIAM L. FOX

SHOOTING AT SIGNS

A trio of bicyclists pauses at the edge of the blacktop, standing just on the other side of the white line that marks the transition from pavement to shoulder, the latter a liminal area that is not quite road, not quite land. The three figures, each clad in nylon windbreakers and high-impact composite helmets, peer upward at a panel of petroglyphs carved into the desert varnish on the sandstone of a Utah cliff. Just below the carvings a relatively fresh scar reminds us that the land is always changing—as does the relative position of the incised figures. They were made hundreds or thousands of years ago when the ground was ten or twelve feet higher than it is today. Erosion and road-building have lowered the elevation of the foreground. The photograph bears with it the requisite irony that images of the inhabited wilderness must disclose, yet we sense that the photographer Terry Falke is revealing something more than a clever juxtaposition of the Neolithic with the New Age.

The spread of photography and the systematic exploration of the world's deserts, including those of the American West, occurred at roughly the same time, the optical technology extending and fixing our viewpoint of arid environments through a series of powerful tropes. In the case of Egypt, viewers in the nineteenth century were presented with the ruins of an ancient culture that seemed mythically powerful, remnants of a people who were once able to lift up and transport the largest cut stones in the world. On the other side of the globe, America's Southwest was represented as untrammeled wilderness, a desert hostile to humans and shaped by natural forces. The only visible antiquity in the American deserts was geological, not cultural. Explorers in the New World transferred the exotic nomenclature of Egypt to American landmarks, applying names such as Karnak and Pyramid to prominent ridges and outcrops. This linguistic prestidigitation allowed them to claim an American link back into time immemorial that exceeded that of the European roots in ancient Egypt and Greece.

Timothy O'Sullivan, who traveled with Clarence King's Fortieth Parallel Survey in the late 1860s and early 1870s, was trained on the battlefields of the Civil War by Mathew Brady, and he brought with him both a documentary flair and a constitution sturdy enough to lug a view camera across the sands and up the peaks of Nevada's Great Basin Desert. He established what became an enduring theme in landscape photography of the region, a relatively blank topographical gaze that seemed to present only the geological facts of those features. People, if they were present at all, were allowed a walk-on role only to provide scale in the landscape.

During subsequent decades of that century, photographers were paid to ride the new transcontinental railway routes to promulgate the view that the arid regions were unparalleled opportunities for settlement. They carefully cropped out sand dunes and sagebrush flats, aimed their lenses at every river and water hole they could find, and abetted a land rush that by 1890 had putatively closed the American frontier.

As cities and roads took hold across the West, photographers were next encouraged by their corporate patrons to emphasize the scenic value of the deserts to lure tourists. Organizations such as the Automobile Club of America reproduced images by Edward Weston and Ansel Adams, and concentrated on the scenic climaxes of national parks and what would later be declared wilderness areas. These photographers likewise tended to ignore the presence of the human in the landscape to preserve the notion that you had only to turn around and a pristine wilderness was still available for your pursuit of leisure. In later decades photographers Philip Hyde and David Muench, working through mass-media vehicles such as *Arizona Highways Magazine,* continued to promote the Southwest as a territory with its virtue intact. We looked out across the deserts of North America, the defining landscapes of the American Southwest, and where we had a hundred years earlier thought *wasteland,* we now adopted its cognate, *wilderness*.

This perception was reinforced by the photographers even when they were pursuing their personal aesthetic visions. Adams and Weston, although at times working in the commercial sector, were primarily artists seeking to create highly formalized, even abstract representations of nature. That artists of such renown presented the interior West as an Edenic retreat lent credibility to images by lesser-known photographers in the tourist promotions. As with O'Sullivan, whose work Adams admired, irony seldom if ever raised its head.

As the cities in the arid West began to metastasize past any semblance to common sense, however, the photographers came to rue the loss of open space and the consequent degradation of the environment. Adams, and soon thereafter his counterpart working in color, Eliot Porter, became environmentalists armed with art. Now, instead of framing pictures empty of people to attract tourists to the West, their compositions urged us to value the remaining scenic climaxes by holding them harmless from development. Images by both men were widely published by the Sierra Club during the 1960s in books and calendars, and their pictures became popular icons for the environmental movement. It became, in fact, almost impossible to discuss wilderness or landscape photography in the same sentence as the American West without evoking their names, in particular that of Ansel Adams.

In the 1970s these highly aestheticized images found themselves hanging next to photos by a younger group of artists with a revisionist approach. Edward Ruscha cruised the Sunset Strip and produced a foldout view of the streetscape as if he were William Henry Holmes making topographical panoramas of the Grand Canyon in the 1880s. Ruscha's work helped inspire William Jenkins at the George Eastman House in Rochester, New York, to curate a 1975 exhibition titled "New Topographics," an exhibition in which Robert Adams and Lewis Baltz gave us a view of the West based on housing developments and industrial parks. Frank Gohlke turned trees into telephone poles, and O'Sullivan's rocky outcrops were supplanted by chemical plants.

The legendary exhibition turned American landscape photography on its head by demonstrating that it was possible to redirect the deadpan approach of Timothy O'Sullivan to what was now unmistakably an altered landscape. In reality, of course, the American Southwest had been inhabited for more than 12,000 years by a succession of peoples who left behind only a few artifacts in caves, arrangements of rocks in the landscape ("geoglyphs" so subtle that most anthropologists walked over them), and the petroglyphs and pictographs we loosely refer to today as "rock art." What altered our perception was that the inhabitation was now visible, and it wasn't pretty.

The rephotographic work done by Mark Klett, Ellen Manchester, and others in the "Second View" project later that decade confirmed that the change had taken place on a wholesale level. The team put photographs by O'Sullivan and William Henry Jackson side by side with those made from the same vantage point a hundred years later. It was only a short step from their comparative surveying—two separate photographs next to each other, one with a view of a landscape, the next with an overlay of suburbia—to a single photograph in which the two occurred simultaneously. And that is analogous to what Terry Falke would do starting in the 1990s.

Falke, who was born in San Antonio, Texas, in 1950, had been a photographer since the early '70s. When doing graduate work at Bard during the early 1990s, Falke had already taken wholeheartedly to the cool and distanced objectivity of the New Topographics, given up black-and-white photography for color, and cultivated a taste for the ironic in the work of Robert Frank, Garry Winogrand, and more recently in Joel Sternfeld's *American Prospects,* a body of color work made primarily during the 1980s.

The disjunction between what we expect to see and what is really in front of us is a prime tenet of irony, a word that came increasingly into vogue during that decade. The root for *irony* in Greek means "feigned innocence," and was a classical debate technique whereby a speaker appeared to offer up a weak position to trap his opponent into revealing the intentions behind his position. It was and remains a rhetorical method for uncovering a deeper truth while appearing naive. In contemporary photography, that meant taking what appears to be a documentary photograph within which two or more elements find themselves unexpectedly face-to-face.

When Ansel Adams photographed his winter sunrise scene in the Owens Valley of California, the eastern ramparts of Mount Whitney standing snow-covered in the background, he included a horse to define the foreground scale and to balance the grandeur of the geology with a touch of life. In Falke's framing of a similar scene *(Winter Sunrise, Sierra Nevada, California, 1998),* the foreground is occupied by an electrical substation surrounded by poles and wires. It's a deliberate play on the Adams photo, of course, an allusion to the lessons of rephotography, and a handsome picture in its own right that gives us a pang of conscience.

It's not just a surreal juxtaposition that creates irony but a poignant one that produces a wry smile at what seems an immediately familiar absurdity. Joe Deal, Len Jenshel, and Joel Sternfeld are among other photographers who have observed the landscape in this manner, all of them using a slightly distanced vantage point from their subjects to allow the incongruity of the surrounding situation to become apparent. In Falke's photograph of the Sierra Nevada, he has adopted the strategy whereby he selects an element that would normally be hidden, or at least be of secondary importance, and with a straight face brings it into the foreground, making it equal or superior to what we would expect to be the primary subject. Thus the substation becomes the primary object, allowing the subject to be the contrast that emerges between it and the landscape.

It's a mistake to draw too straight a line through this narrative and say that it leads right to Terry Falke and his photograph of the cyclists standing underneath the petroglyphs. Ansel Adams and Edward Weston, for example, did occasionally include traces of the human. Weston's 1937 *Hot Coffee, Mojave Desert* confronts us with a huge and crudely made cup and saucer in front of a creosote bush, what was then at least a humorous, if not actually ironic, image of roadside advertising. And Adams in his 1950 book *The Land of Little Rain* used railway lines and highways running across the desert as compositional devices. Likewise, the flat journalistic style of photos taken in the dust bowl by Dorothea Lange during the Depression prefigured the New Topographics forty years later.

There is, in fact, another entire category of photographic images that exploits the flip side of this preference, pictures that couple overtly female sex and masculine power with the landscape to sell us consumer goods. Think of models draped in the latest Italian fashions reclining on sand dunes, or SUVs racing across dry lake beds in a cloud of alkali dust. But overall, it is the images without reminders of human presence in the Western landscape that the public most desires, and that have been most widely reproduced, a predilection still evident today as we peruse calendars at the supermarket. It is Falke's contrarian nature that finds him pointing his lens at the road signs perforated with bullet holes. Although the results contain humor, they are not merely a play on photographic conventions, nor simply a series of visual witticisms.

To return, then, to Falke's *Cyclists Inspecting Ancient Petroglyphs.* By extending to us the privilege of seeing both the cyclists and the object of their wonder, by stepping back and allowing us to see how the land has been altered under the feet of both the ancient figures and the modern ones, the photo lets us see more of the picture than the subjects can. Falke brings together the mythical anthropomorphs of the past with the almost science-fiction-like presence of the riders—an unexpected juxtaposition that conflates two disparate time periods. It could be a cheap shot—irony can turn to condescension very quickly, as if we're in on the joke, and you, who live inside the frame of the photograph, are not. But we quickly realize that is neither his intent, nor is it an adequate response on our part. Instead, we share the wonder of the cyclists at the same time we're noting the multiple incongruities. And that is a revelation, the complicated nature of what is inhabited.

Almost always Falke is working an angle. A guardrail, highway, river, sign, or headlights in the dark cut across the picture frame, leading us ever so gently but relentlessly into the deeper middle ground of the landscape, where place suddenly slips back into space; where culture edges up to nature and then fades away. But something is happening in the far background. A hotel stands behind the trees on the far shore of the lake. Houses are nestled under the hills across the river. At other times the order is reversed, but to much the same effect: a stuffed moose stands in a foreground cage with its door wide open, the desert in the middle ground with the edge of a suburb as a backstop. Often, it is the diagonal that brings to the foreground the very element that creates the irony, yet points to something more.

Among Falke's recurrent themes is what he calls "Native America Anglicized," the appropriation of the mythic West by Anglo commerce. Imitation tepees are constructed out of pressboard as roadside advertising signs, and bulbous objects with huge eyes that allude to totem poles abut a gas station in Gallup, New Mexico. It's not just how objects in space are arranged in the desert that provides irony, but also the rearranging of history.

The Native American photographs are also inevitably about how we relate to the landscape, no matter who we are, Navajo or Northern European. *Leaving Navajoland, Arizona* presents one of those strong diagonals in the foreground, a fallen sign that thanks us for having visited and urges us to "return for more memories." The sign points at the fence, beyond which lie the scenic wonders of canyonlands on the horizon. The supports for the sign, a fading salmon pink meant to evoke adobe and the color of the land, are made of plywood and just beginning to warp. Our memories are disabused of romance, and we're aware of the entropy that is everywhere and inevitably visible in the desert.

Another theme threaded by Falke through his work is that of the wilderness mitigated and mediated, a concern that appears frequently in work by artists who have spent much of their time camping in the public lands that they photograph. One of Falke's best-known images, *Mitchell Butte, Utah/Arizona Border, 1995,* shows the rock tower lit by the romantic glow of low sunlight. Framing the butte is an artificial sunshade under which two benches and a picnic table await occupants. A barbecue and numbers keyed to a tourist brochure stand nearby. Clearly, it is not enough for us just to admire the view; we are told by the highway engineers and park personnel where to sit, and the order in which we should learn about the wilderness that is displayed in front of us and framed by the amenities.

Wilderness, a word like the terrain for which it stands, is a temptation. We want to think that it exists in opposition to all our screwups, a refuge from human foibles. It is true that you can find places to sit in the desert Southwest where you won't see anyone else, at least for a stretch of time. But there's no place you can go where no one else has walked before, no place where you can escape the contrails of jetliners thirty thousand feet overheard, and no place not claimed by someone else, whether a private property owner, an Indian tribe, or the federal government. Wilderness is not exactly an illusion and can be found anywhere—Elliot Porter once said that he could see it in the weeds at the edge of a road—but the word doesn't always mean what we think it does.

On a planet over which humankind has left physical traces on 83 percent of its surface, the meaning of wilderness has long since shifted from a place to avoid into one that is to be embraced and preserved, a physical and vestigial location that is a metaphor for paradise. We posit wilderness as the opposite of the built environment and construct fierce political battles around the opposition.

As usual, we are a day late and a dollar short.

In 1789 James Watt invented the steam engine. Within the next decade human-generated greenhouse gases began to rise as the industrial age got seriously underway, and humans had begun to alter the entire climactic regime of the planet. Geomorphology—the processes by which the surface of the planet are altered—had hitherto been the province of rain and wind, earthquakes and glacial ice, the kind of processes that O'Sullivan was asked by King to document during their nineteenth-century survey. By the end of the twentieth century we had impounded so much water behind dams that we had altered the very rotation and tilt of the planet itself, and scientists began to say that our most recent geological era, the Holocene, had given way to a new one, the Anthropocene.

Furthermore, areas that we took to be wilderness when they were first explored by Europeans turn out to have been modified by humans for thousands of years. We think of agriculture, which originated in Mesopotamia some eight thousand years ago, as being the first organized activity to shape the land around us. Not so. The Outback of Australia and the Great Plains of America were both deliberately set afire on a regular basis by people thousands of years ago to achieve and maintain desirable levels of productivity for hunters and gatherers. Much of what we take to be the impenetrable rain forest of the Amazon was an anthropogenic landscape created through dikes, dams, and channels for irrigation.

Falke and his fellow ironists insist that we see the landscape as it is—a space we have transformed into place through an ongoing process of increasing complexity. We dig into the land and move it around, erect structures and stories on it, and then make images of the results to suit our varied purposes. A windmill stands in the foreground, a symbol of the ranching that has died out in the arid valleys of the West—and in the background is a gleaming white radio telescope aimed at the sky, evidence of how the land has been recycled. By seeking out such visual contradictions, Falke foregrounds that process of transformation over time. And that, of course, makes him an agent of change, as well.

SOURCES AND FURTHER READING

Castleberry, May, et al. *Perpetual Mirage: Photographic Narratives of the Desert West.* New York: Whitney Museum of Art, 1996.

Foresta, Merry A., et al. *Between Home and Heaven: Contemporary American Landscape Photography.* Albuquerque: University of New Mexico Press, 1992.

Jenkins, William. *New Topographics: Photographs of a Man-Altered Landscape.* Rochester, NY: International Museum of Photography at the George Eastman House, 1975.

Klett, Mark, et al. *Second View: The Rephotographic Survey Project.* Essay by Paul Berger. Albuquerque: University of New Mexico Press, 1984.

Naef, Weston. *Era of Exploration: The Rise of Landscape Exploration in the American West, 1860–1885.* New York: Albright-Knox Gallery/Metropolitan Museum of Art, 1975.

Phillips, Sandra S., et al. *Crossing the Frontier: Photographs of the Developing West, 1849 to the Present.* San Francisco: Chronicle Books, 1996.

Pool, Peter E. *The Altered Landscape.* Reno: Nevada Museum of Art, 1999.

Snyder, Joel. *American Frontiers: The Photographs of Timothy O'Sullivan, 1867–1874.* New York: Aperture, 1981.

PLATES

4 | **Trona, California,** 1998

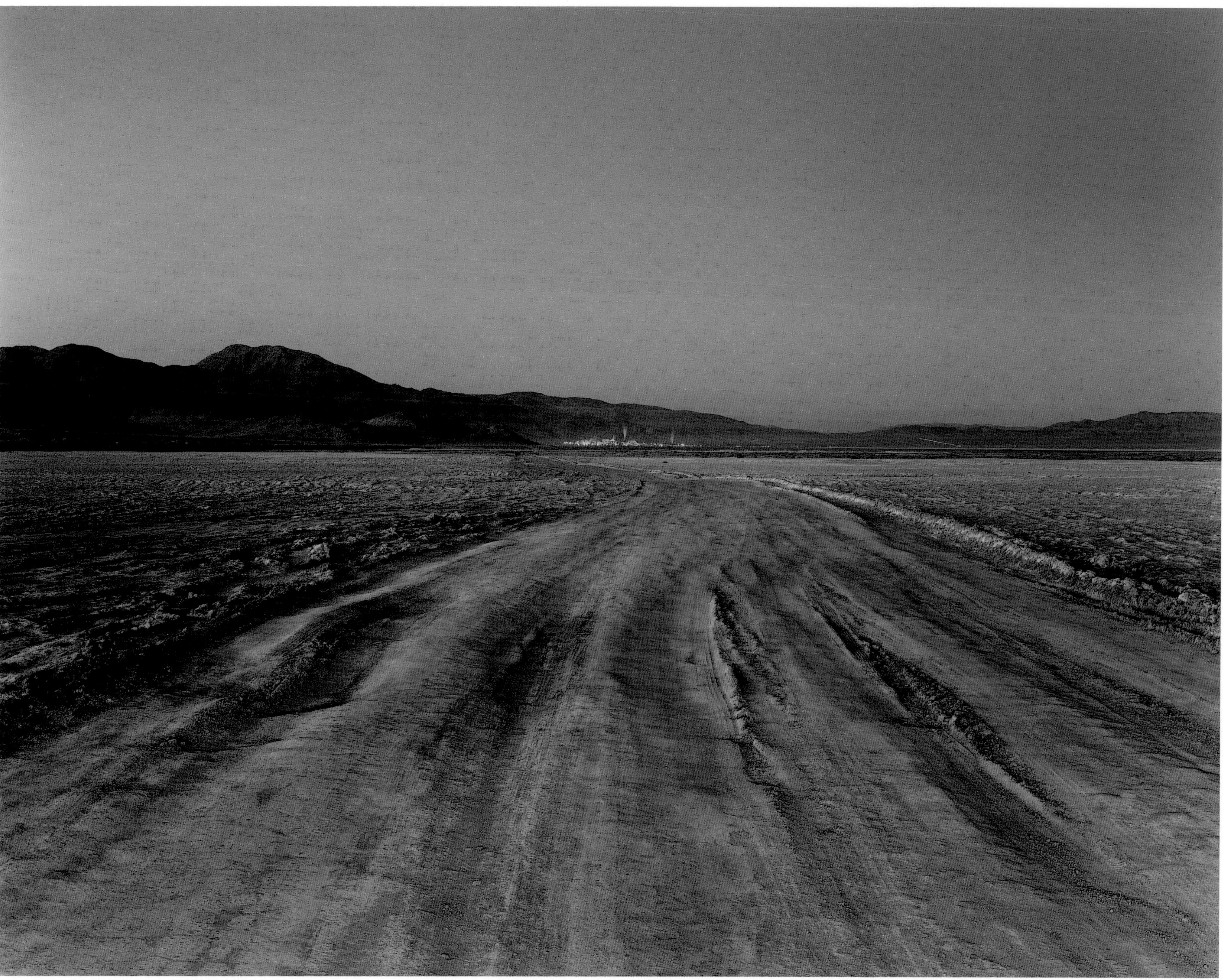

5 | **Glen Canyon,** Arizona, 1997

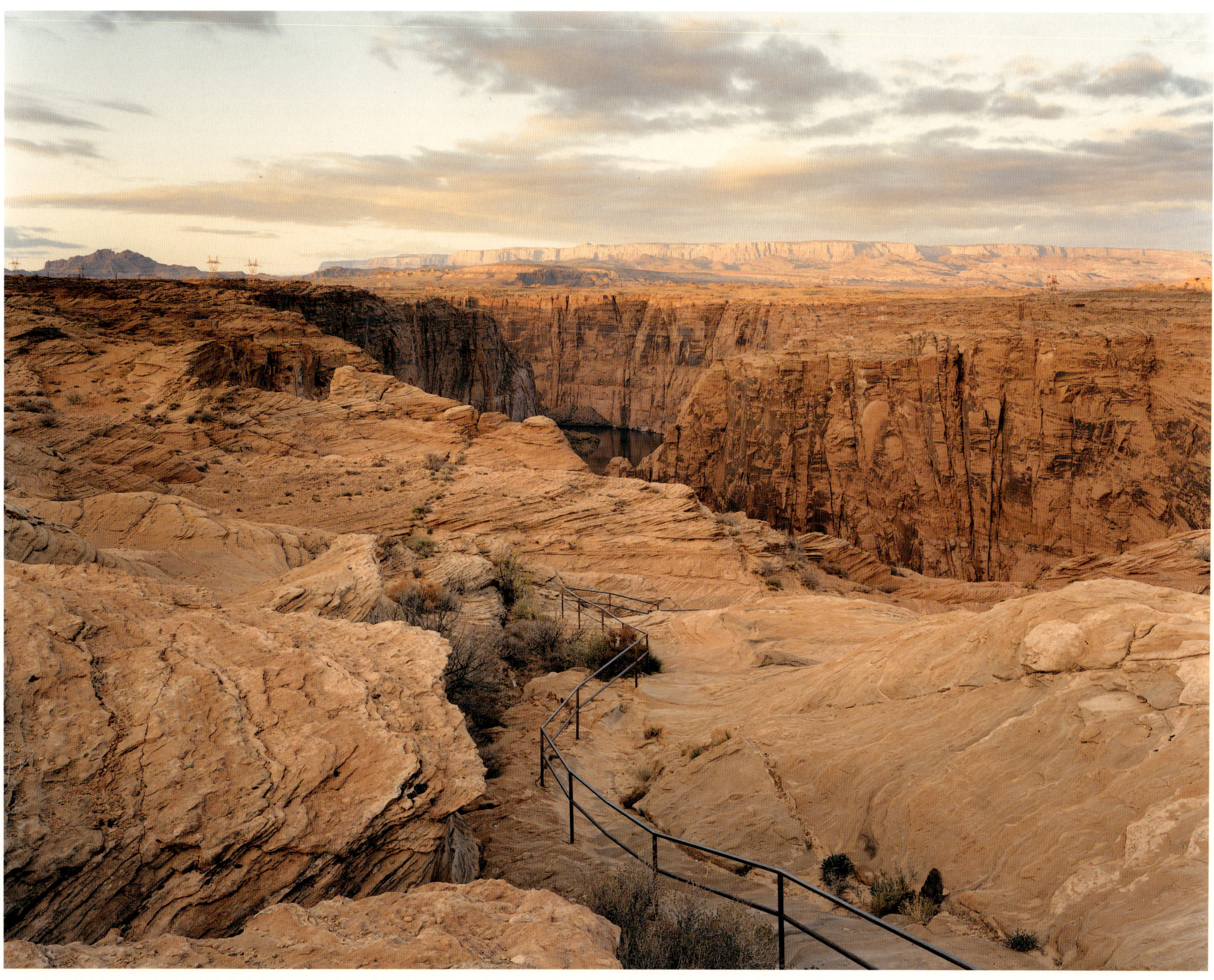

6 | **Winter Sunrise,** Sierra Nevada, California, 1998

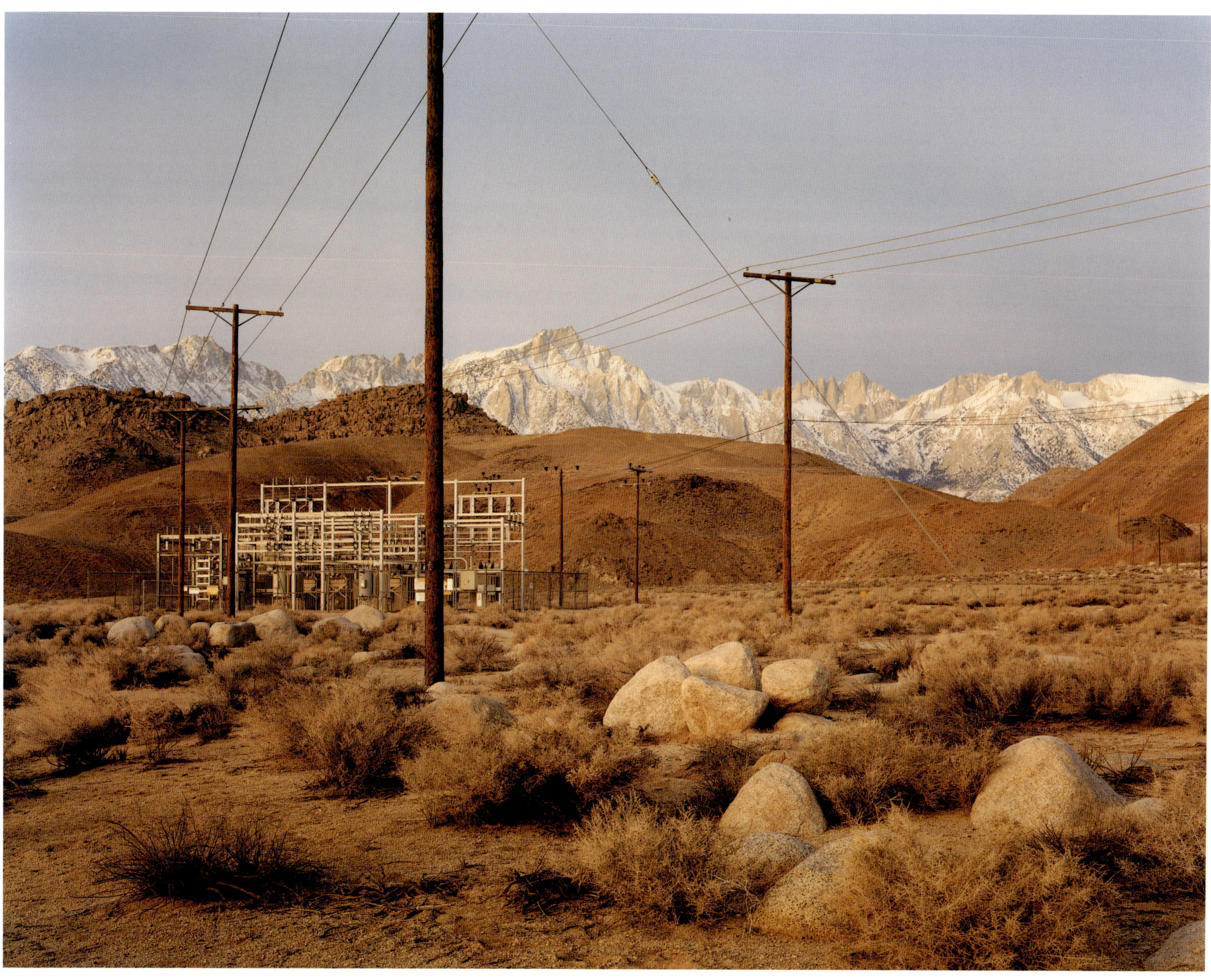

7 | **Standing Rock,** Arizona, 1999

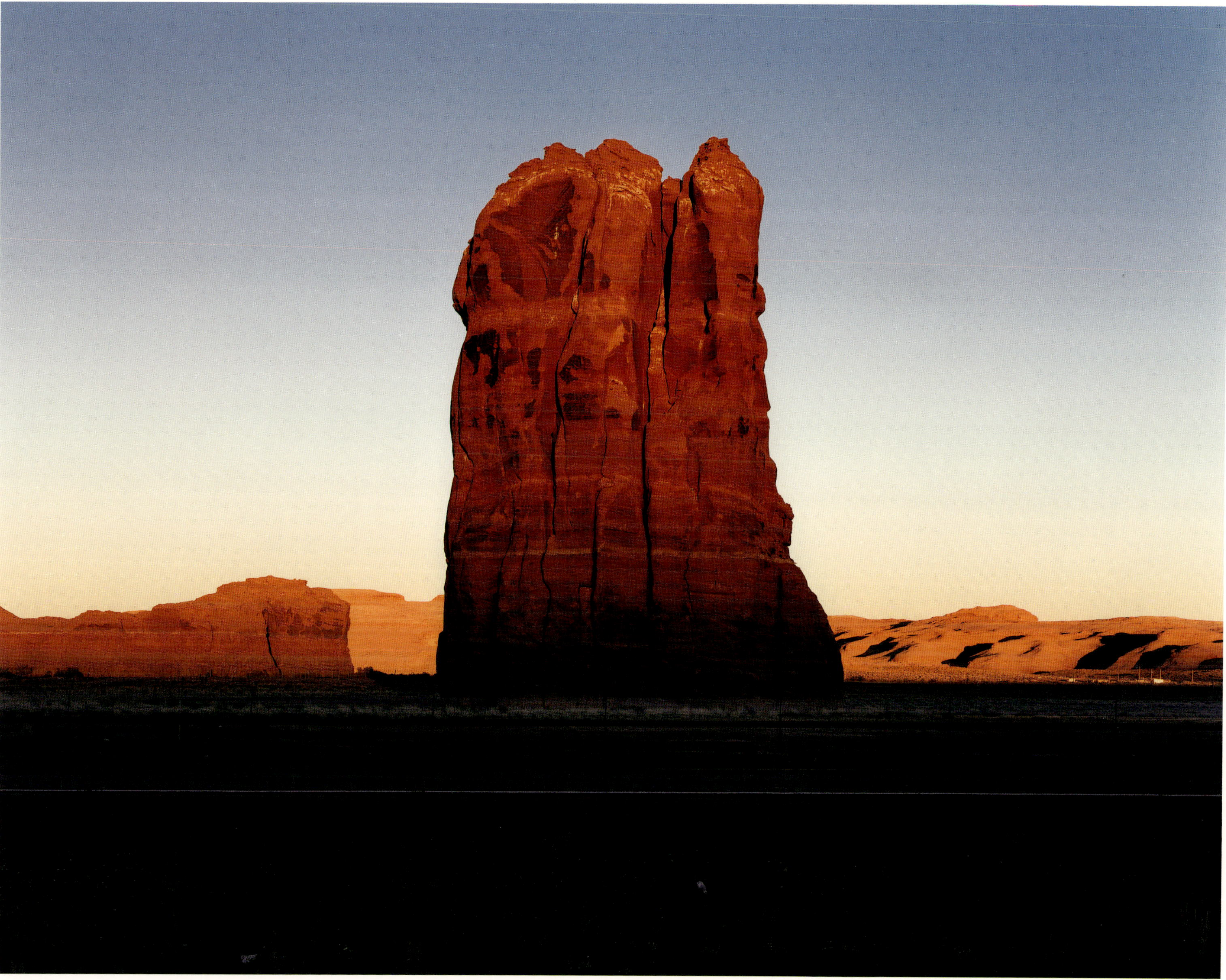

8 | **Campsite with Petroglyphs and Bullet Holes,** Utah, 1996

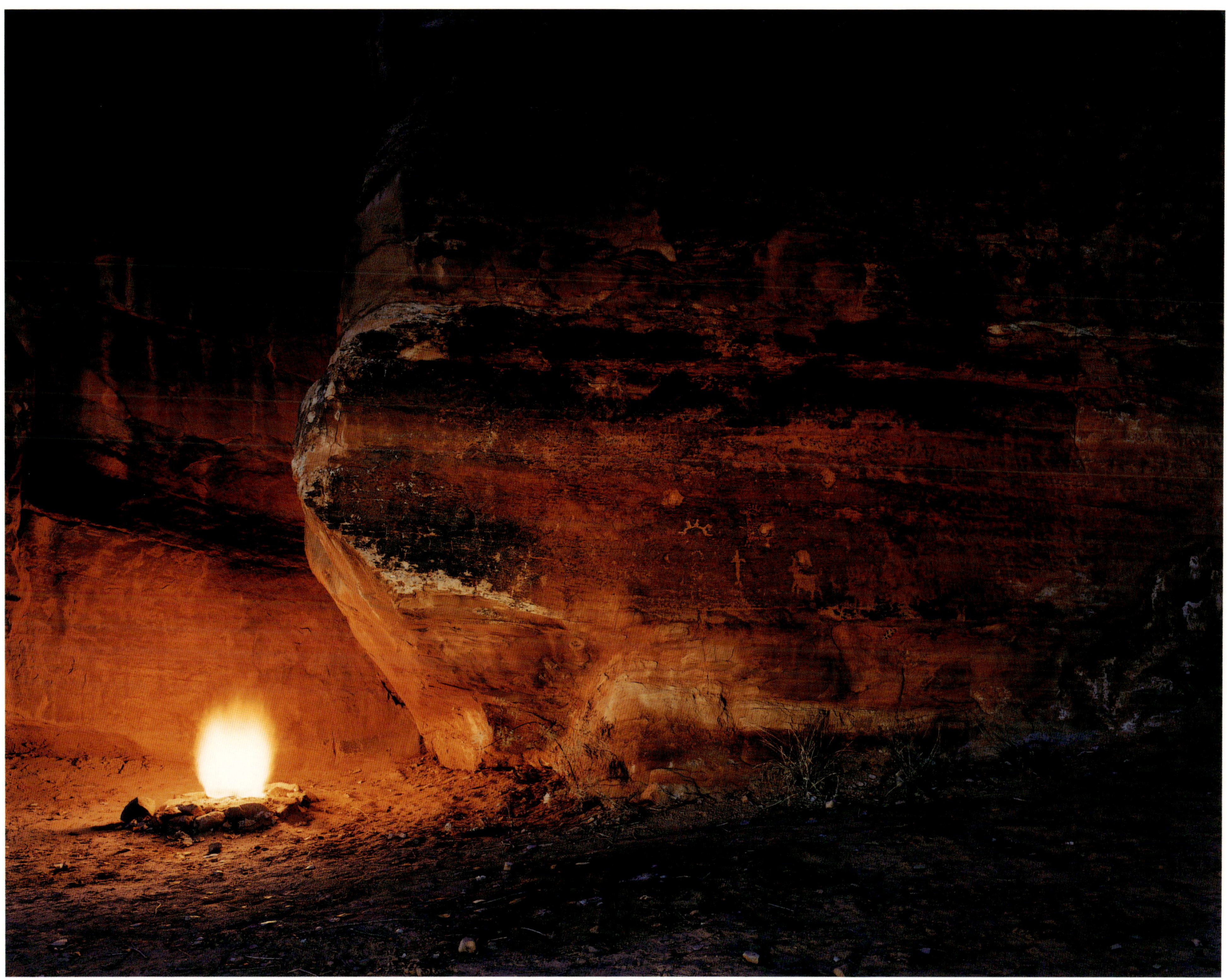

9 | **Shoe Tree,** Nevada, 2001

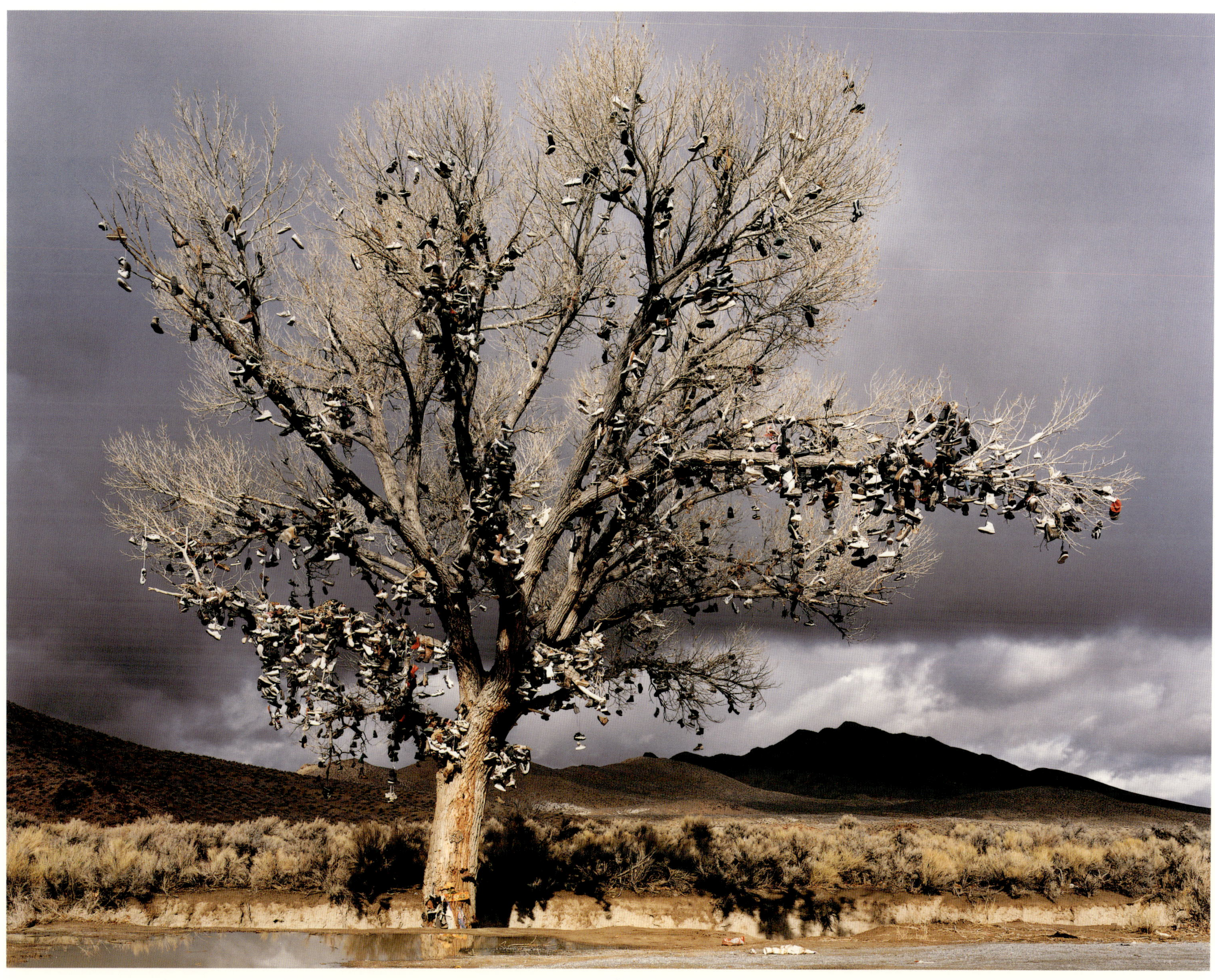

10 | **San Juan County,** New Mexico, 2004

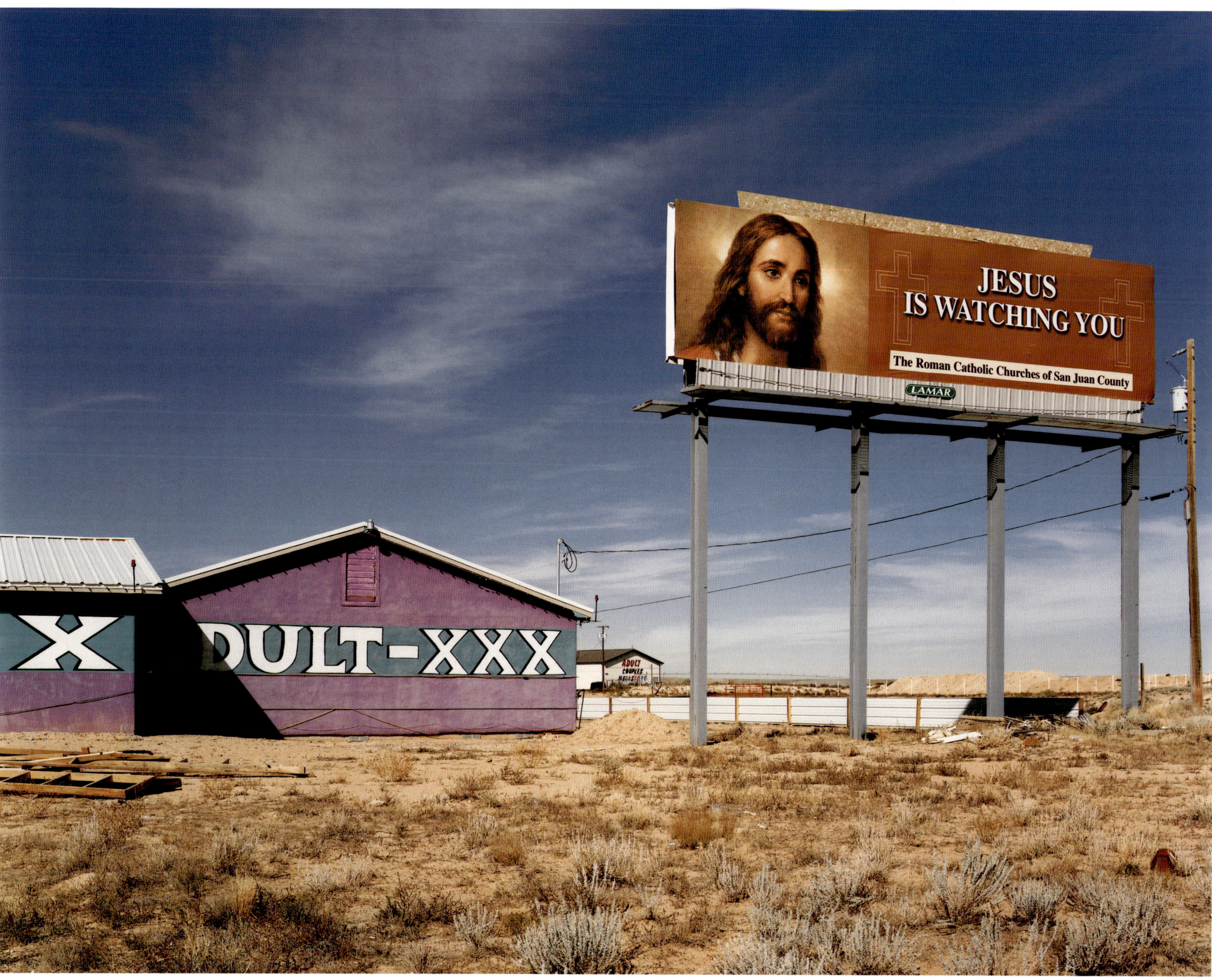
JESUS
IS WATCHING YOU
The Roman Catholic Churches of San Juan County
LAMAR
X
DULT-XXX
ADULT
COUPLES

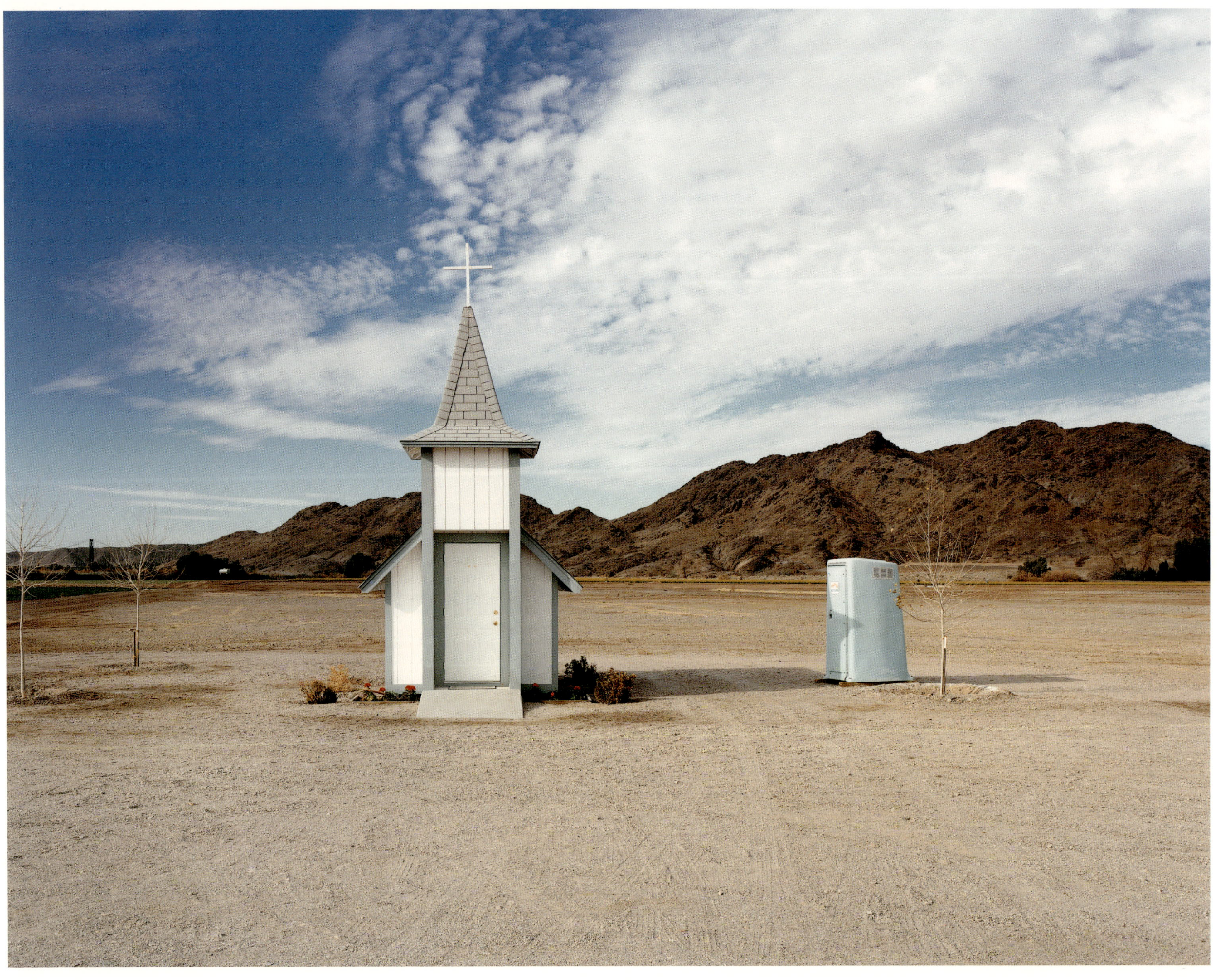

11 | **Chapel,** Arizona, 1999

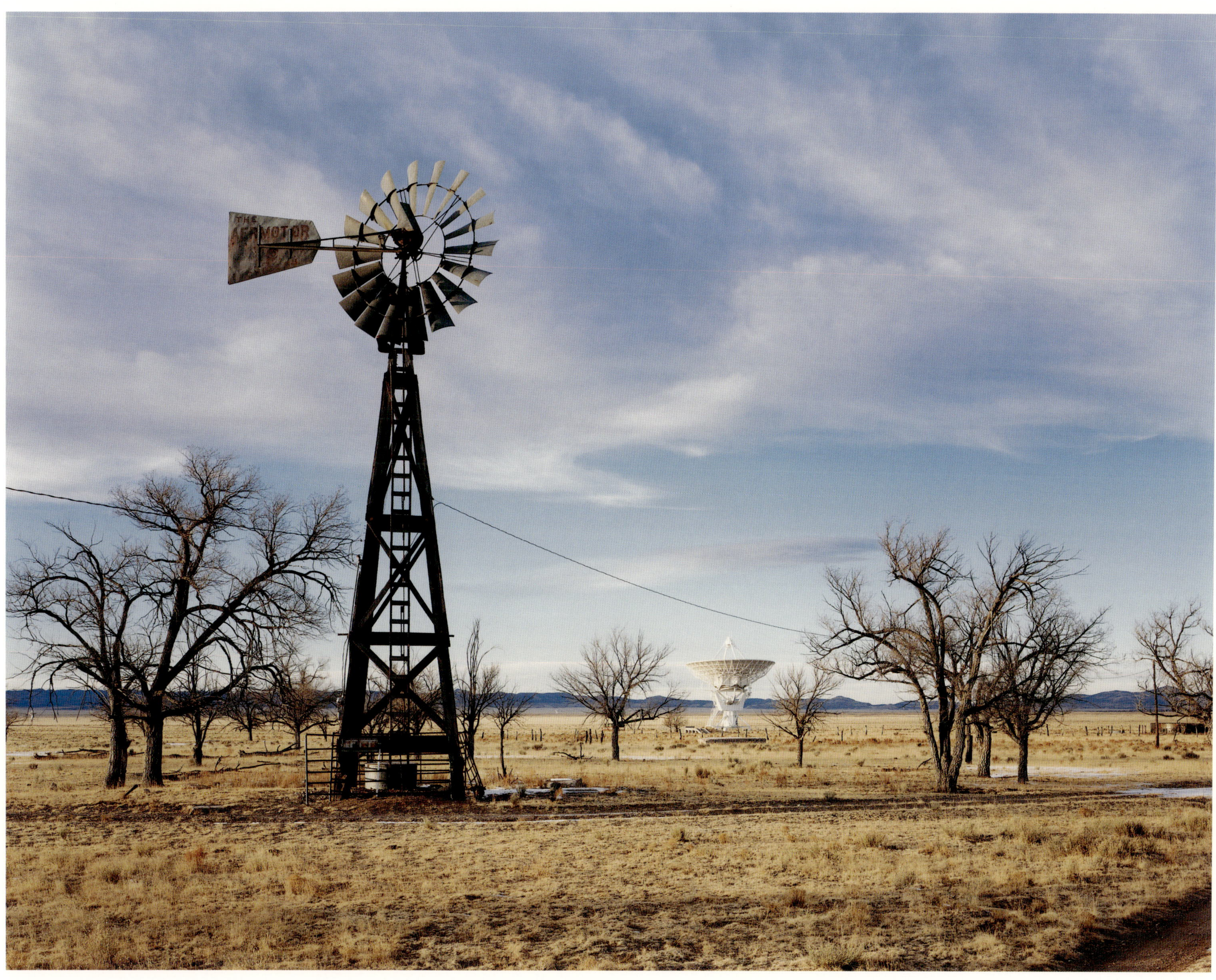

 | **Radio Telescope,** San Agustin Plains, New Mexico, 1999

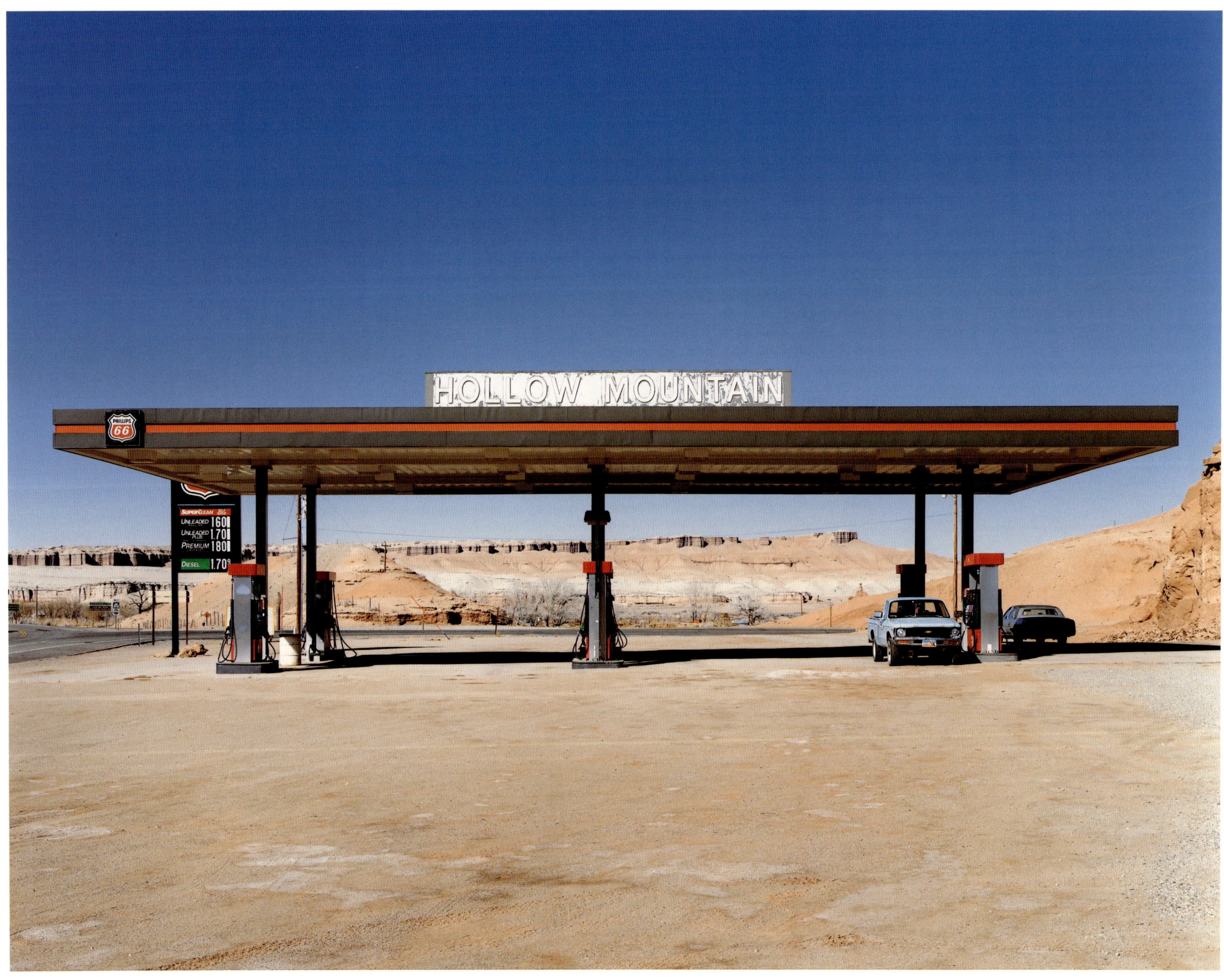

13 | **Hollow Mountain,** Utah, 2003

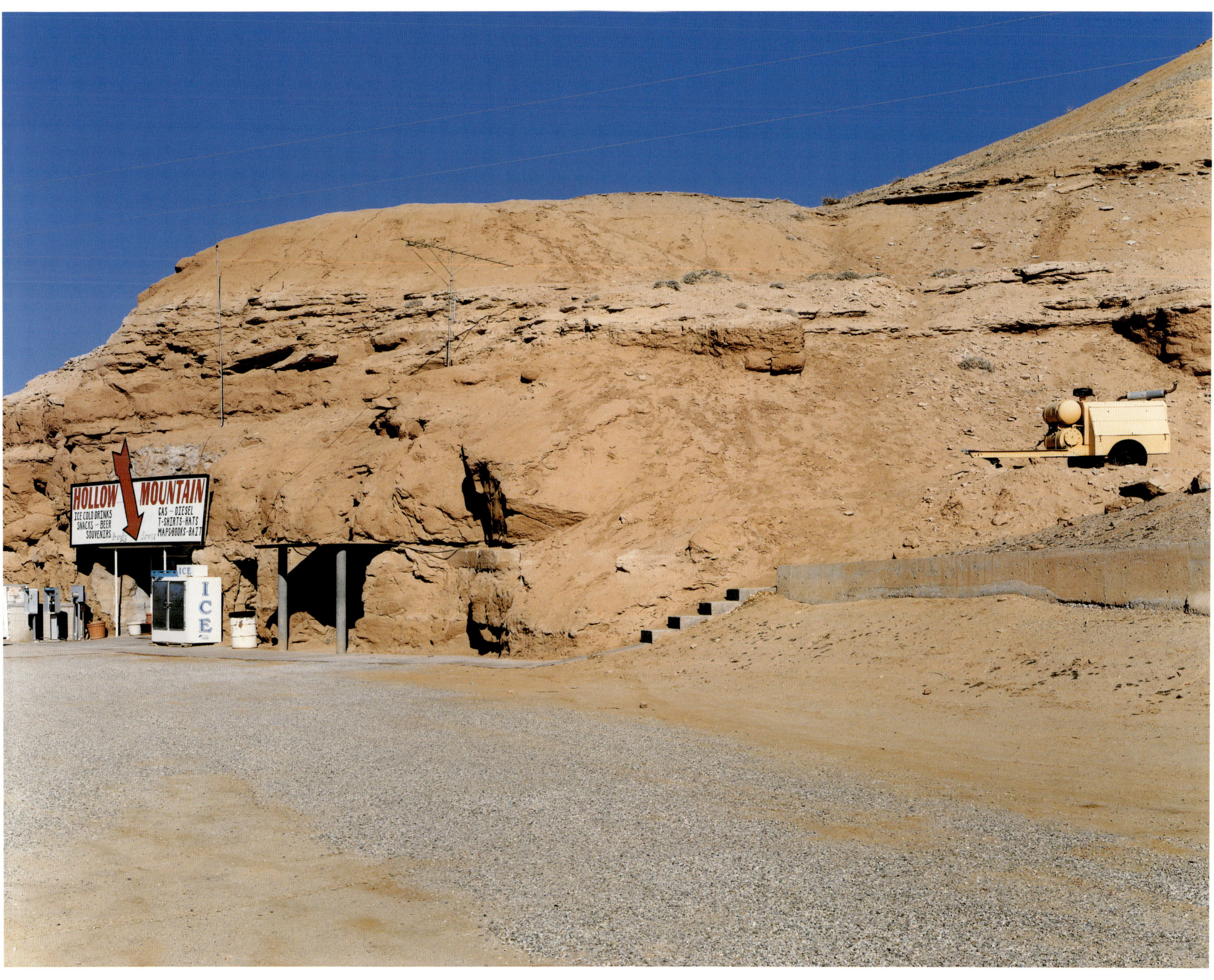
HOLLOW MOUNTAIN
ICE COLD DRINKS
SNACKS ~ BEER
SOUVENIRS
Friendly Service
GAS ~ DIESEL
T-SHIRTS~HATS
MAPS~BOOKS~BAIT
ICE
ICE

14 | **Truck Stop,** Texas, 2001

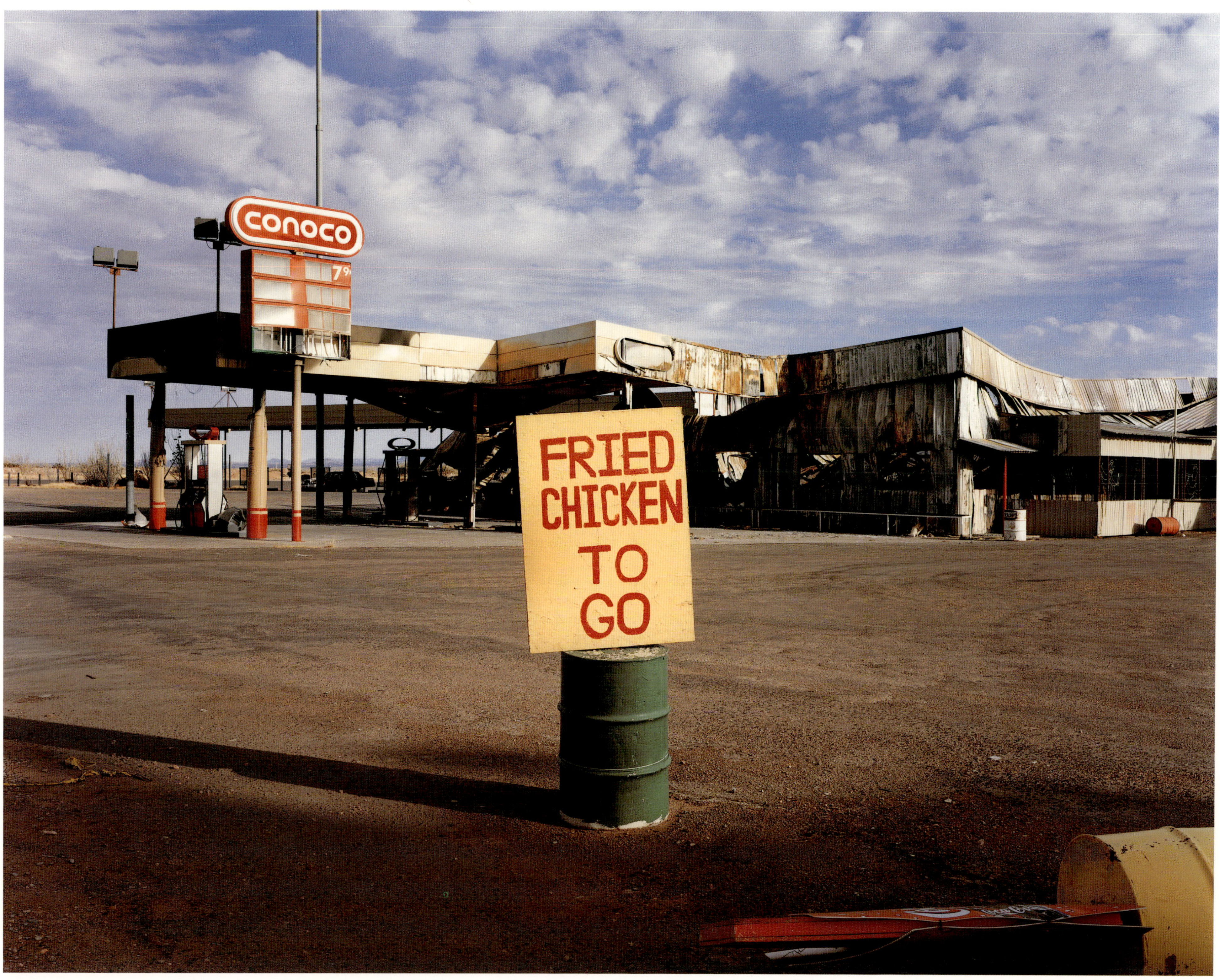
CONOCO
FRIED
CHICKEN
TO
GO

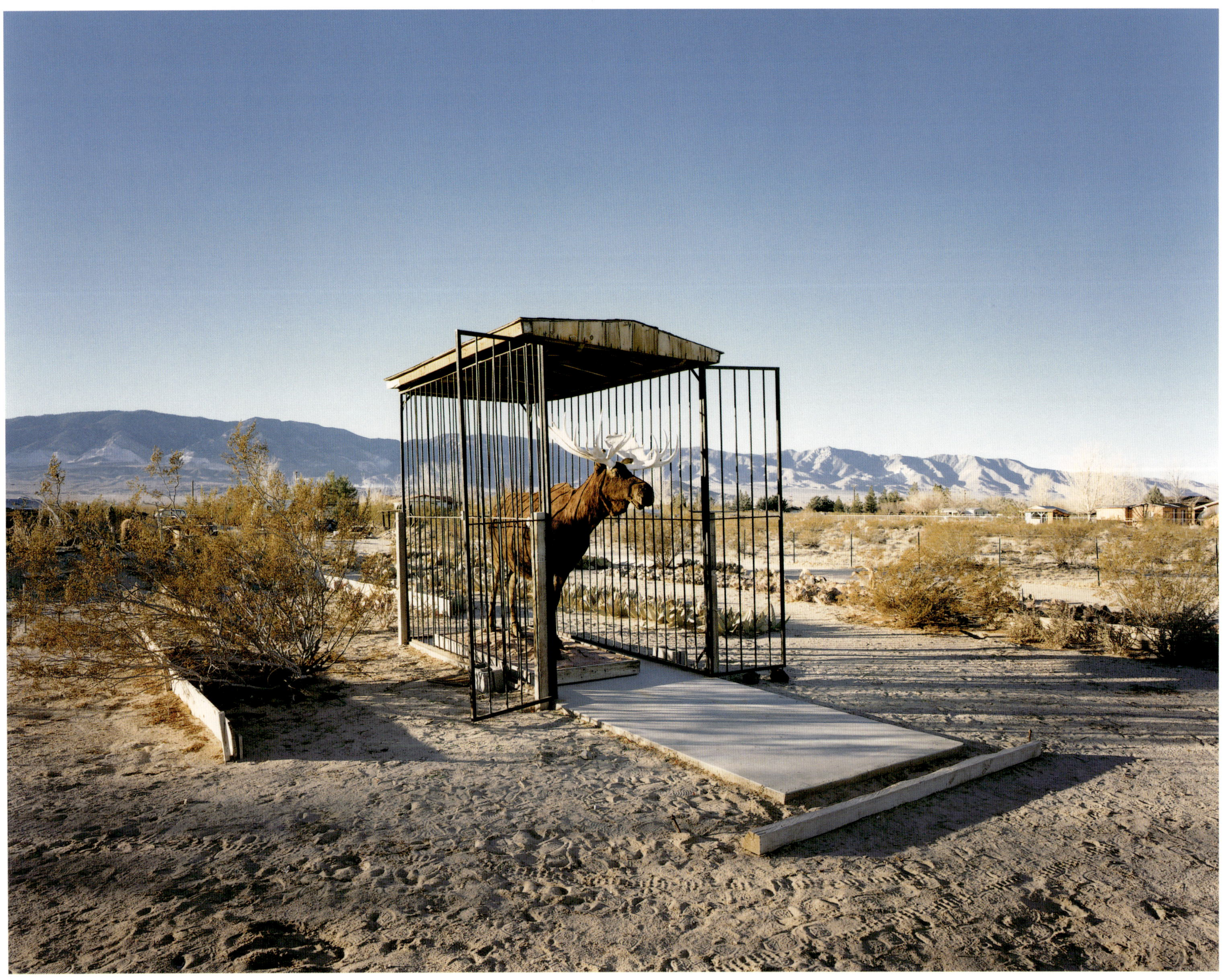

15 | **Moose,** California, 2002

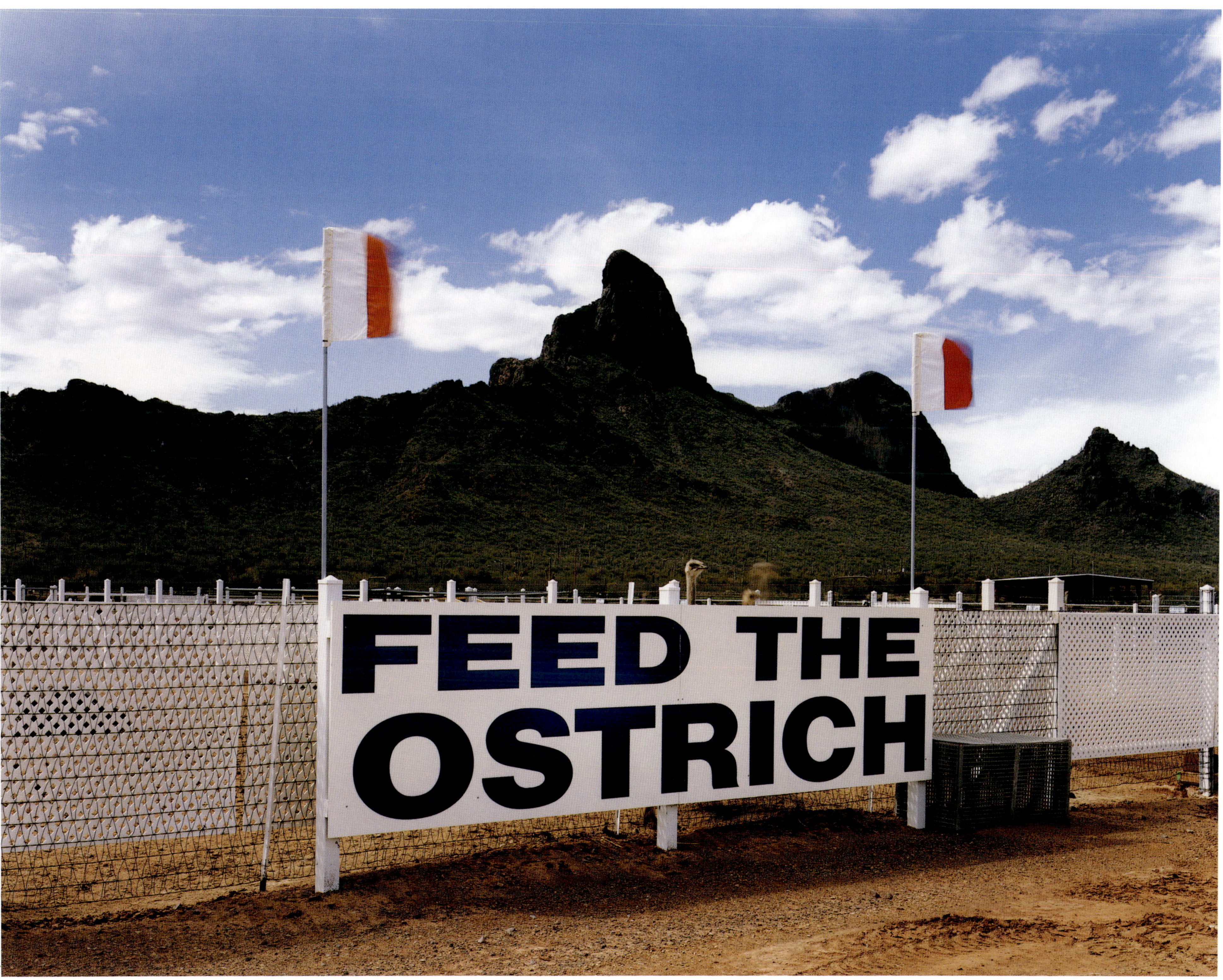

 | **Ostrich Ranch,** Arizona, 2003

17 | **Scenic Overlook,** Utah, 1996

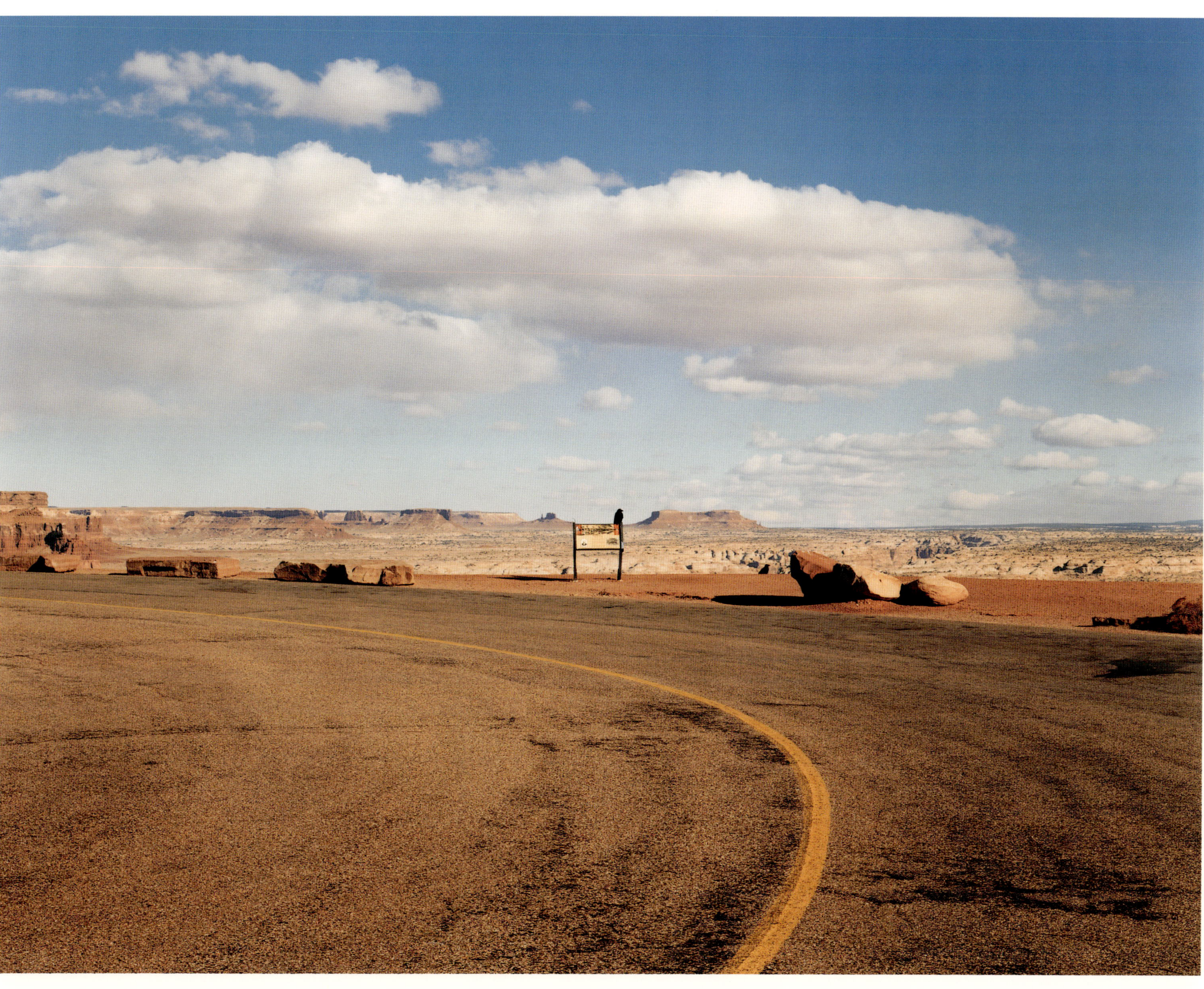

18 | **Privately Owned Petrified Forest Park,** Arizona, 2001

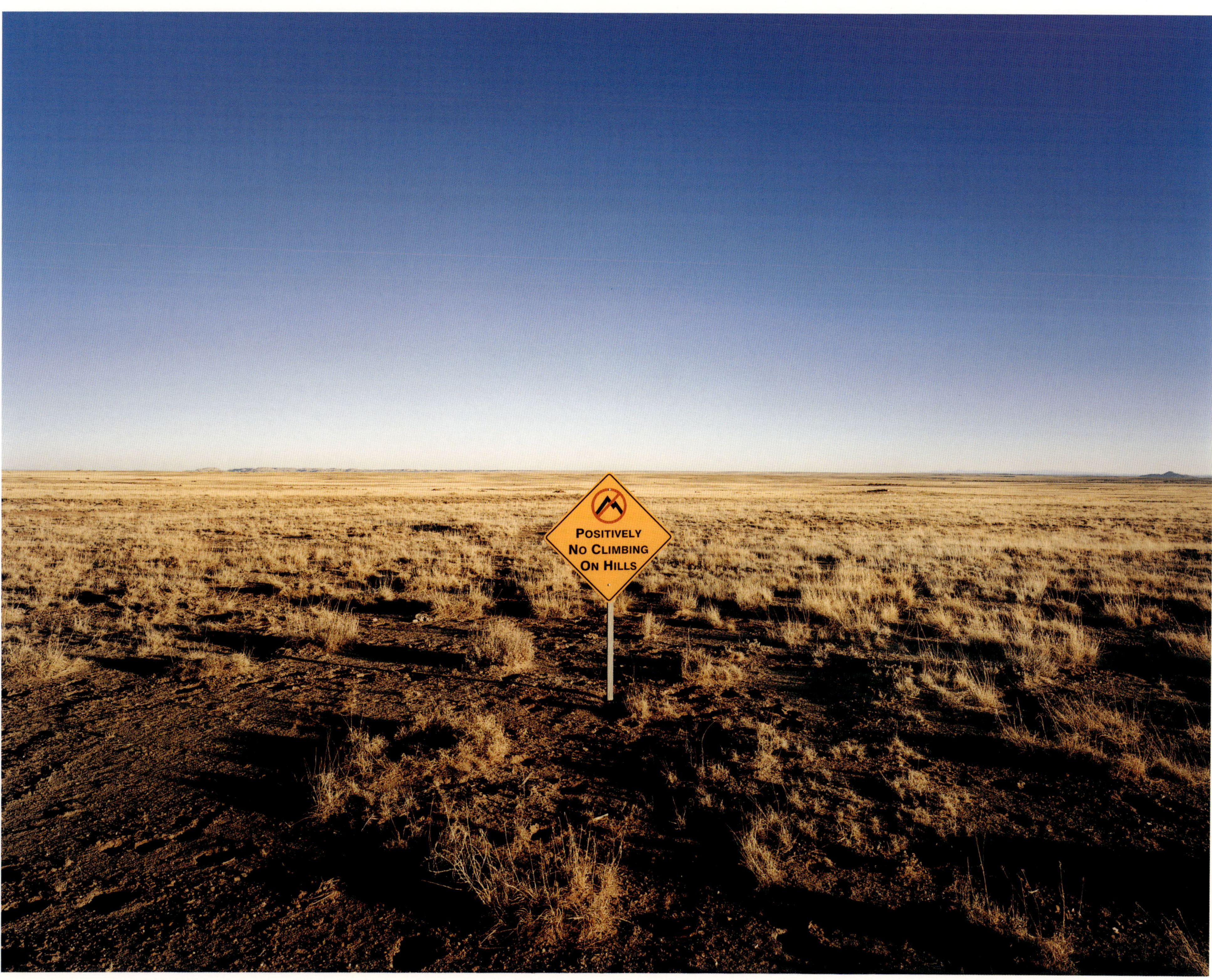
POSITIVELY
NO CLIMBING
ON HILLS

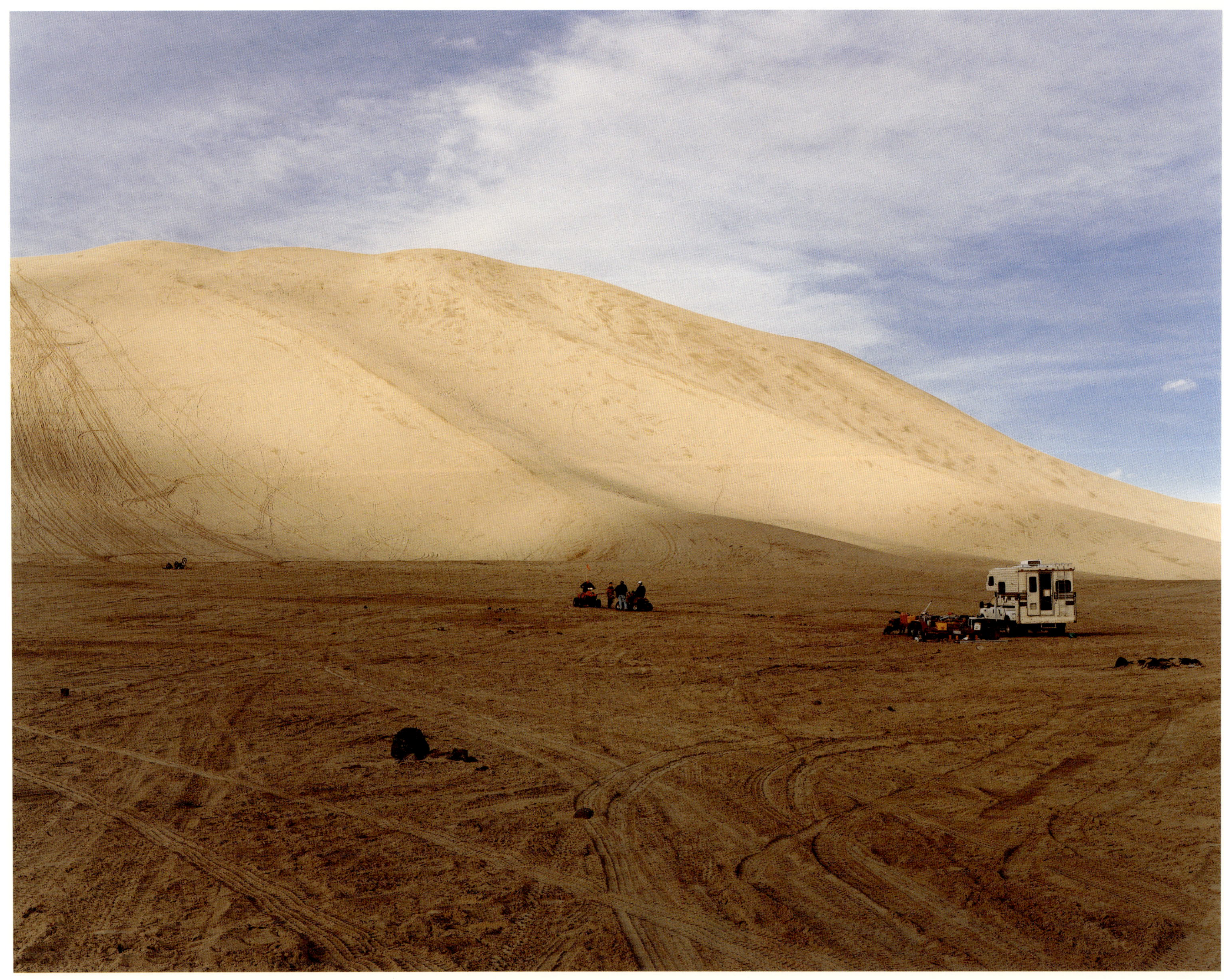

19 | **Sand Mountain,** Nevada, 2001

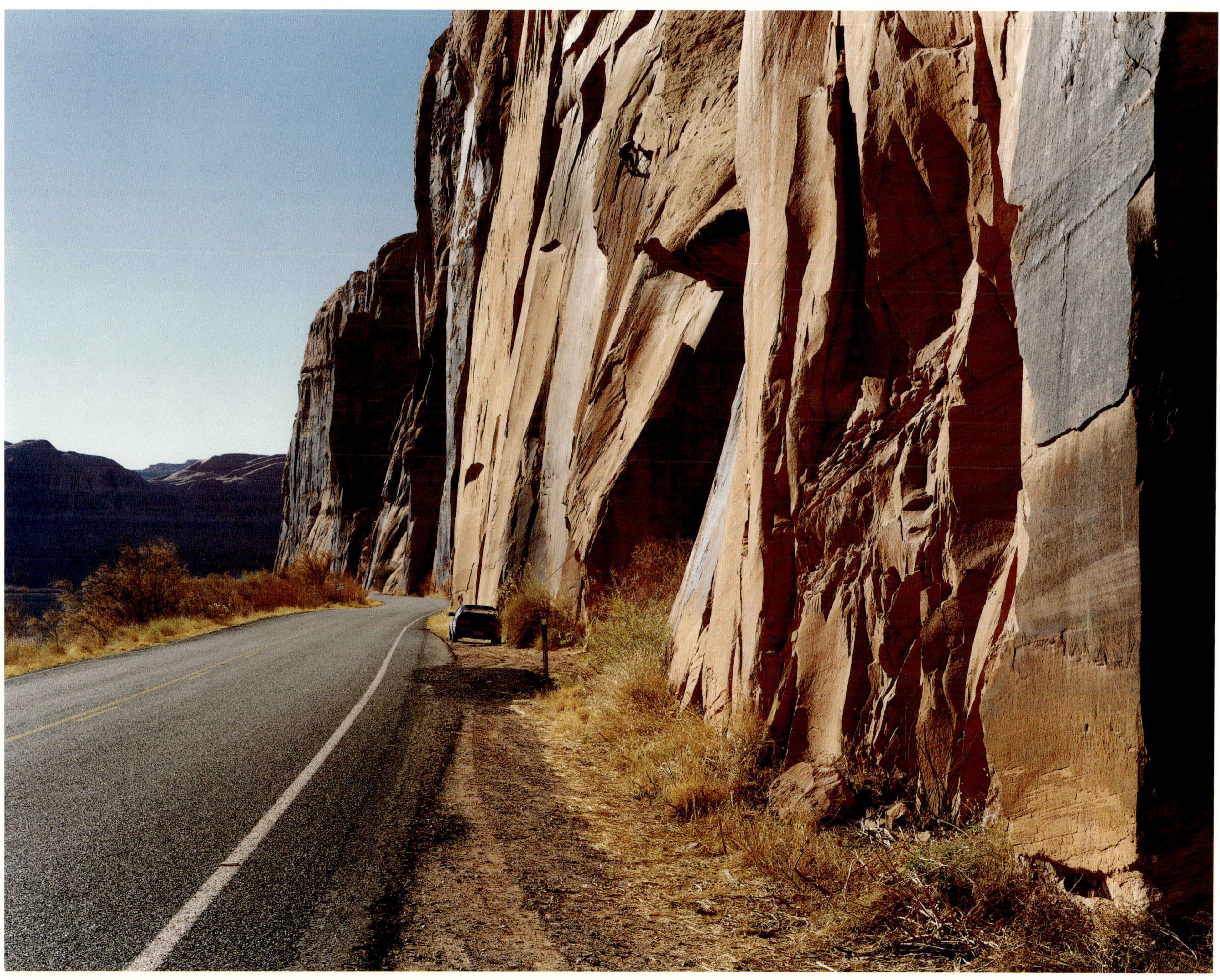

 | **Rock Climber,** Utah, 1997

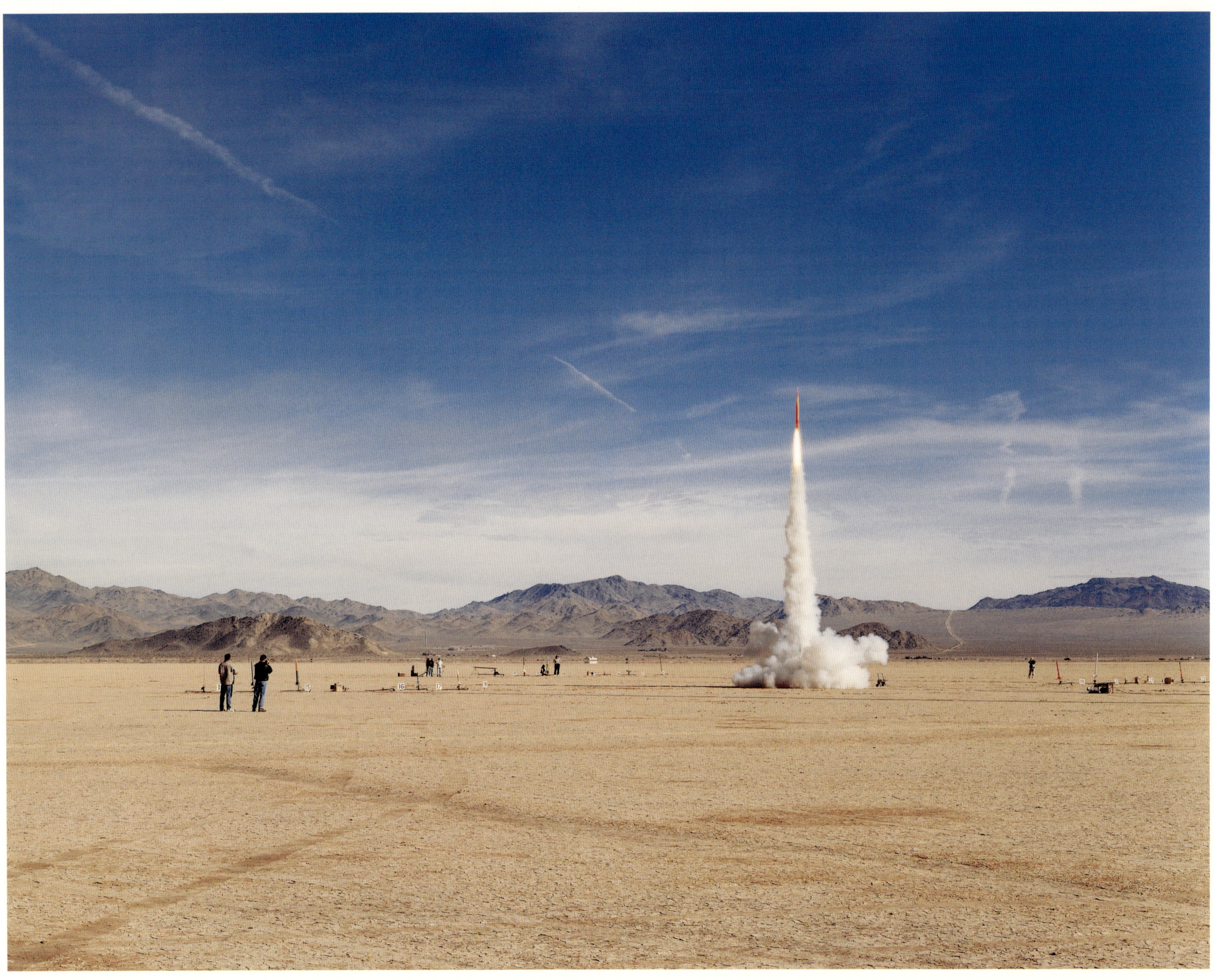

21 | **Amateur Rocket Launch,** Lucerne Dry Lake, California, 2002

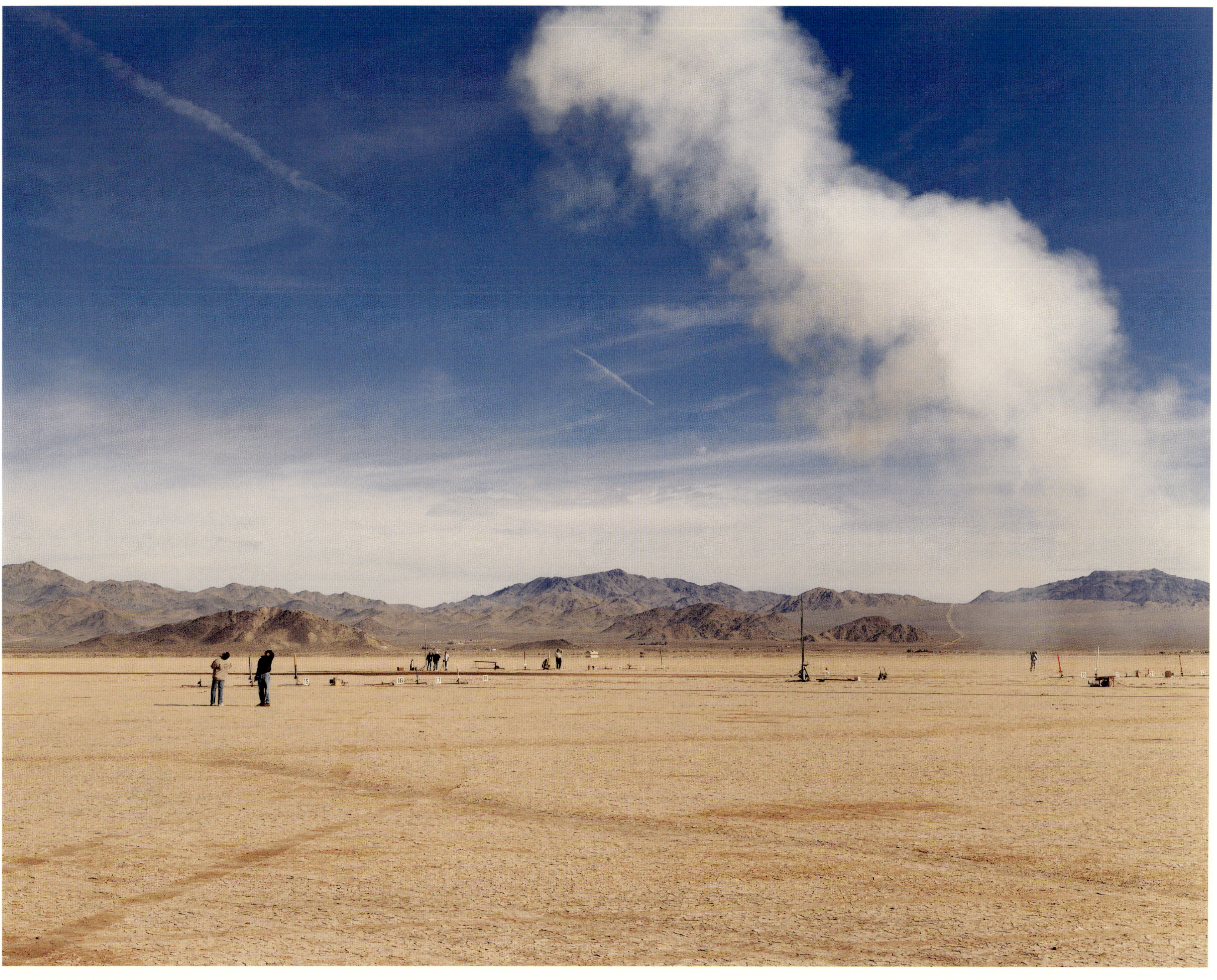

22 | **Trail to Balanced Rock,** Arches National Park, Utah, 1996

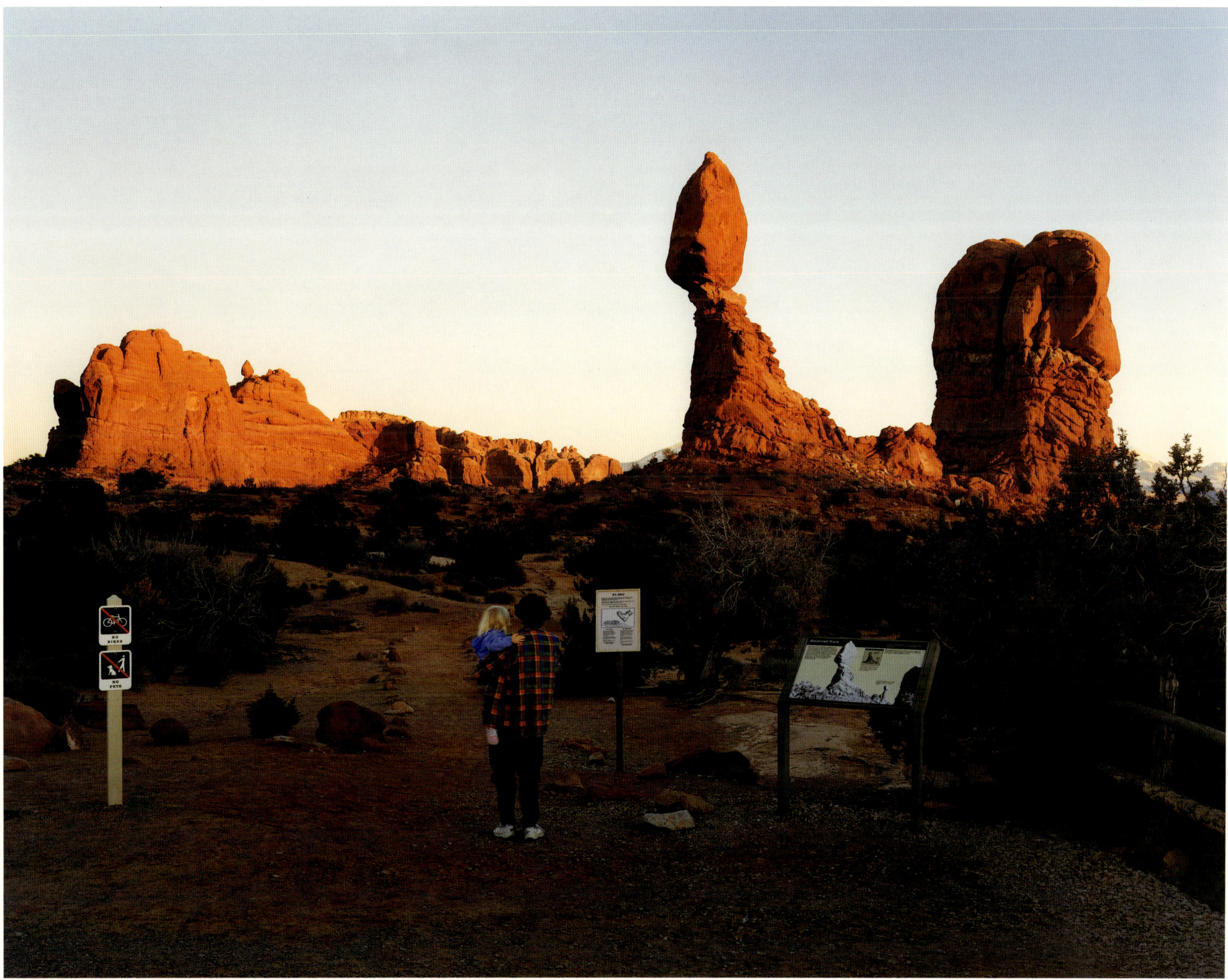
NO BIKES
NO PETS
Balanced Rock

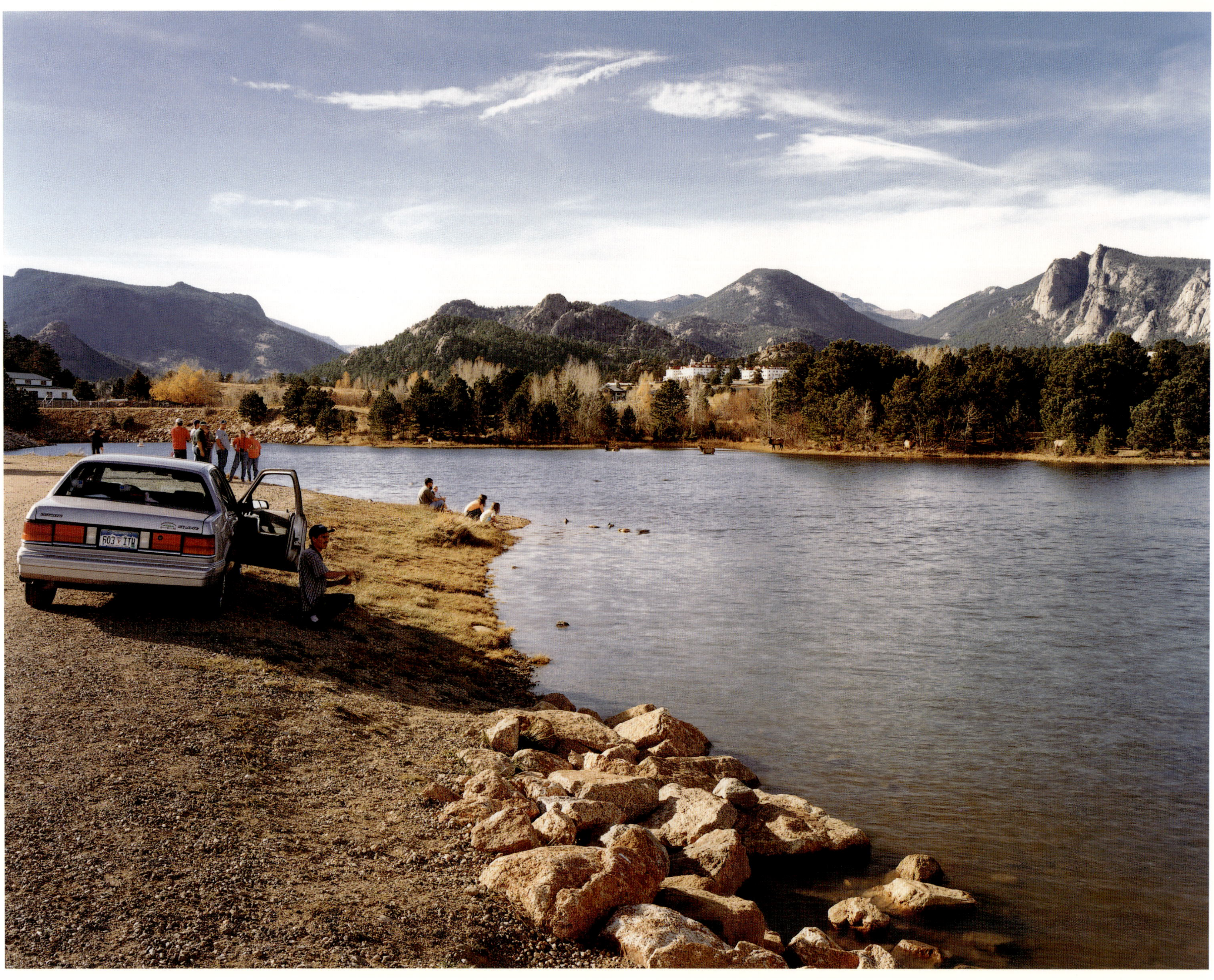

23 | **Lake Estes,** Colorado, 2003

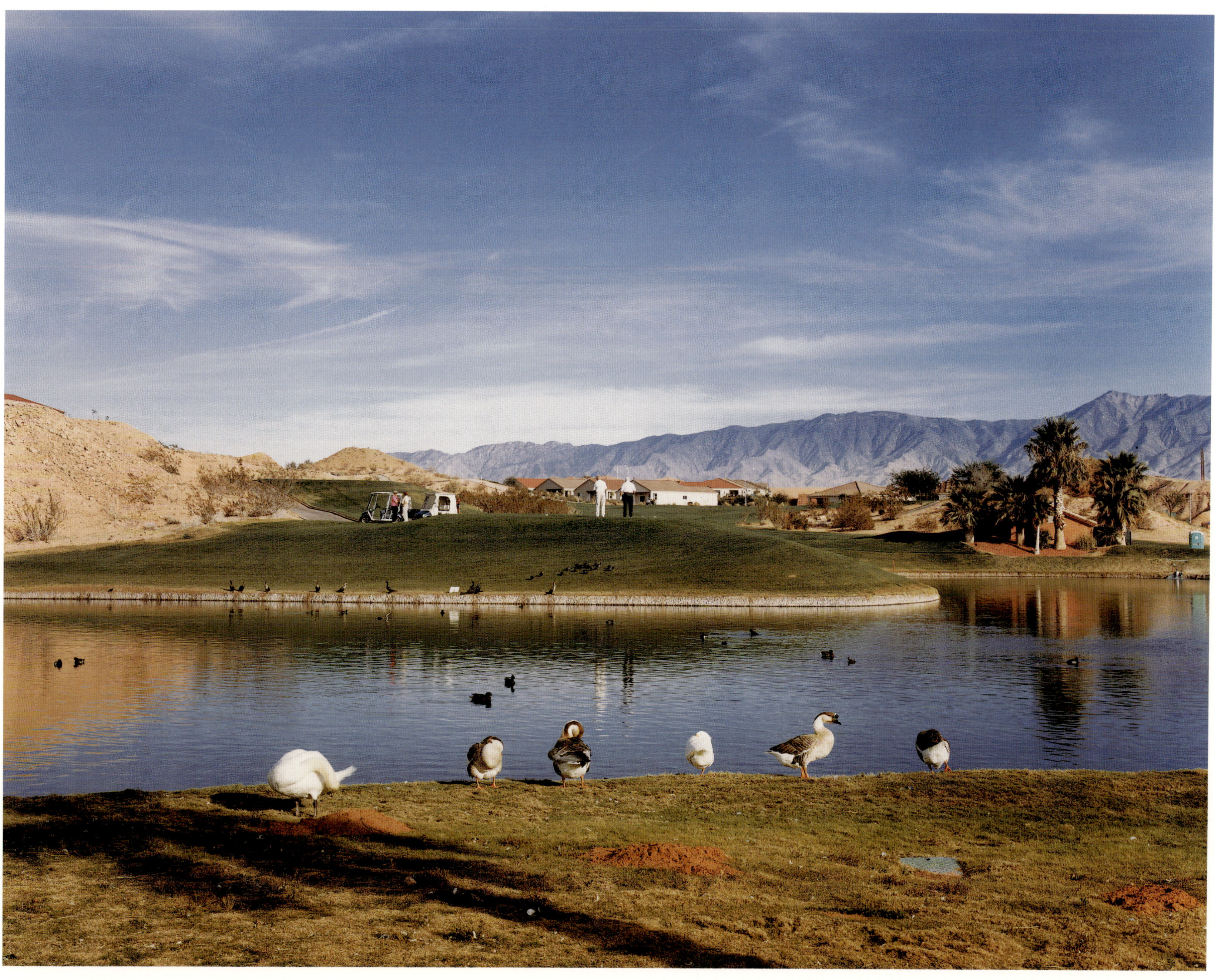

 | **Golf Course,** Mesquite, Nevada, 2003

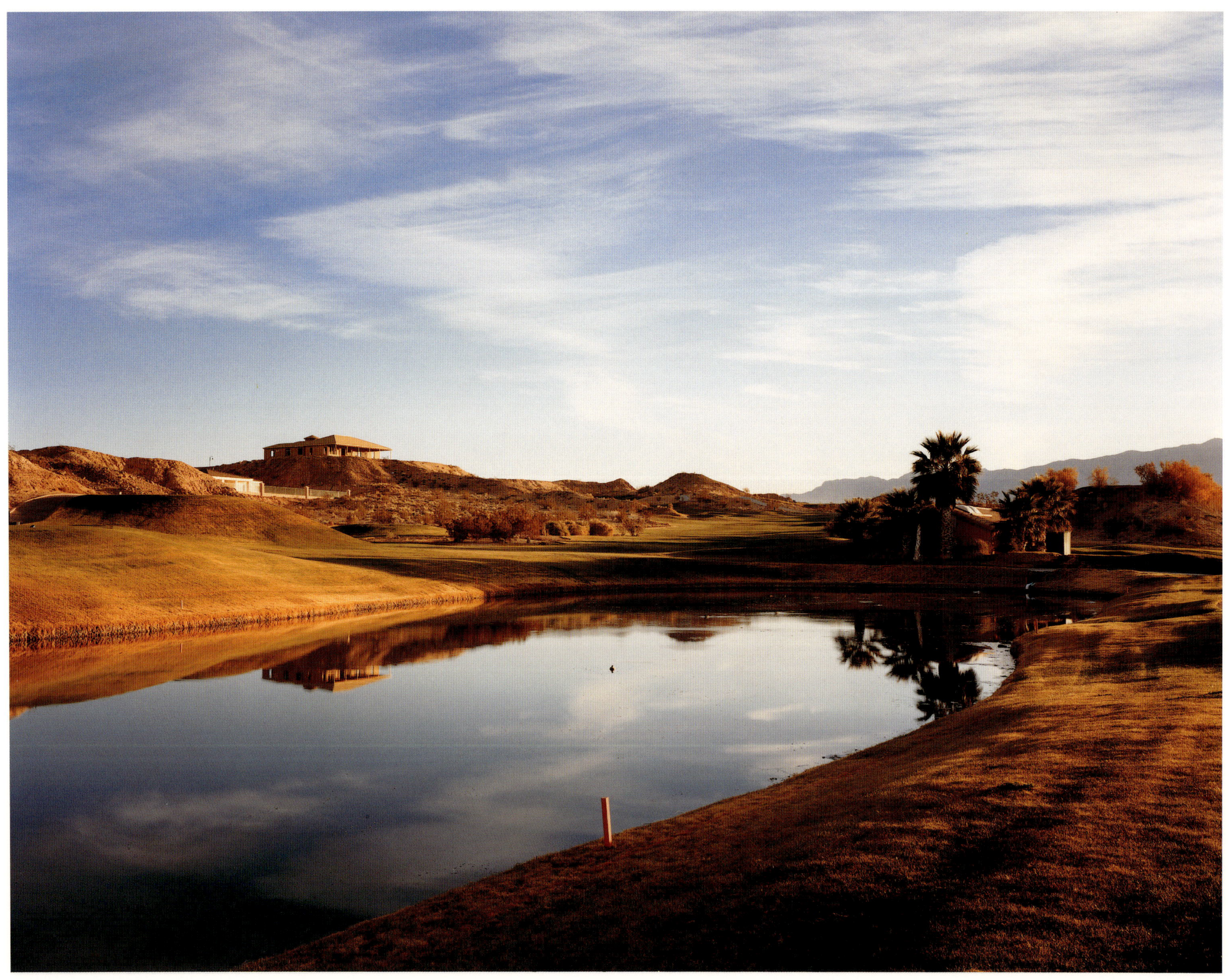

25 | **Golf Course Lake,** Mesquite, Nevada, 2002

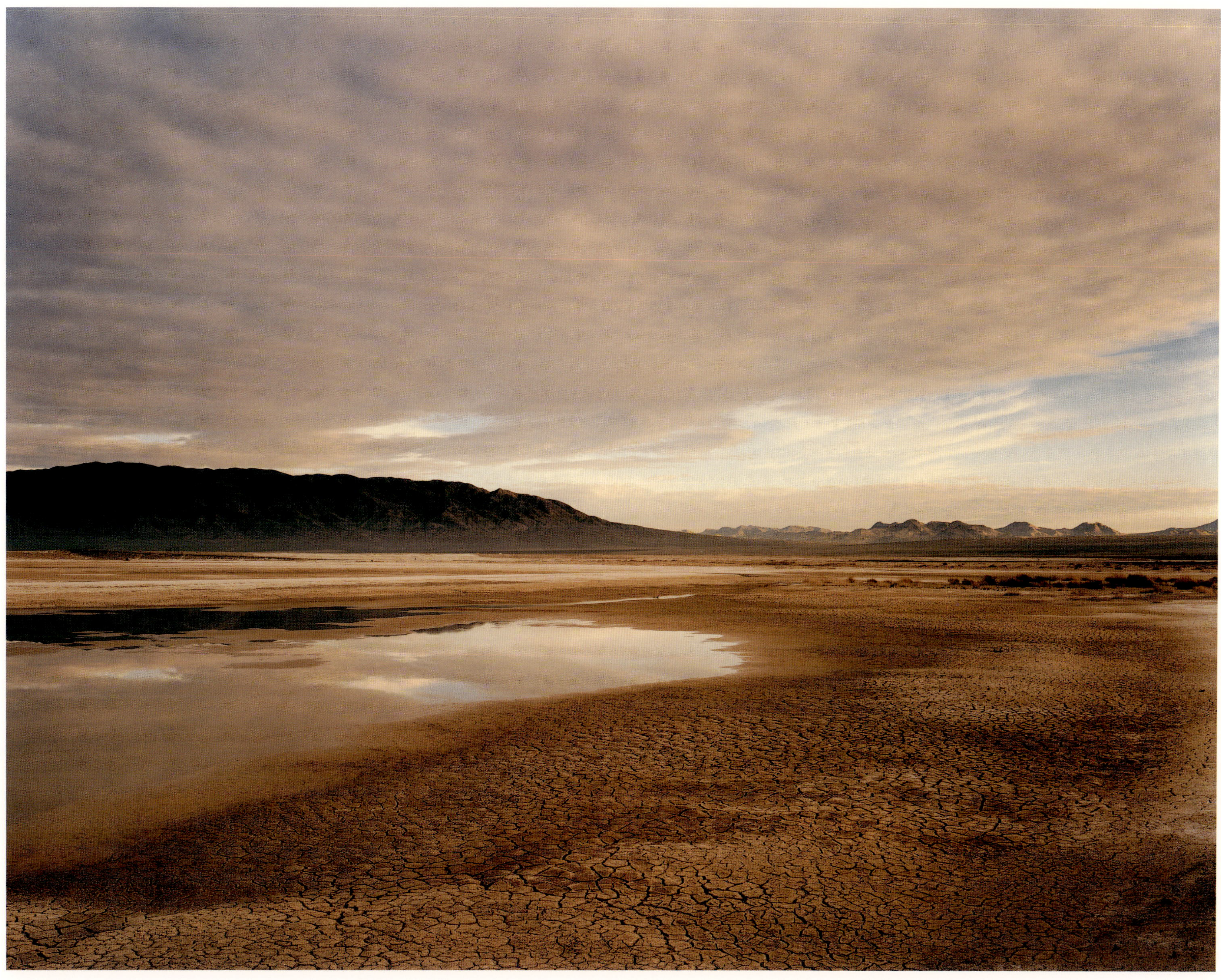

26 | **Evaporating Pond,** Searles Lake Playa, California, 1997

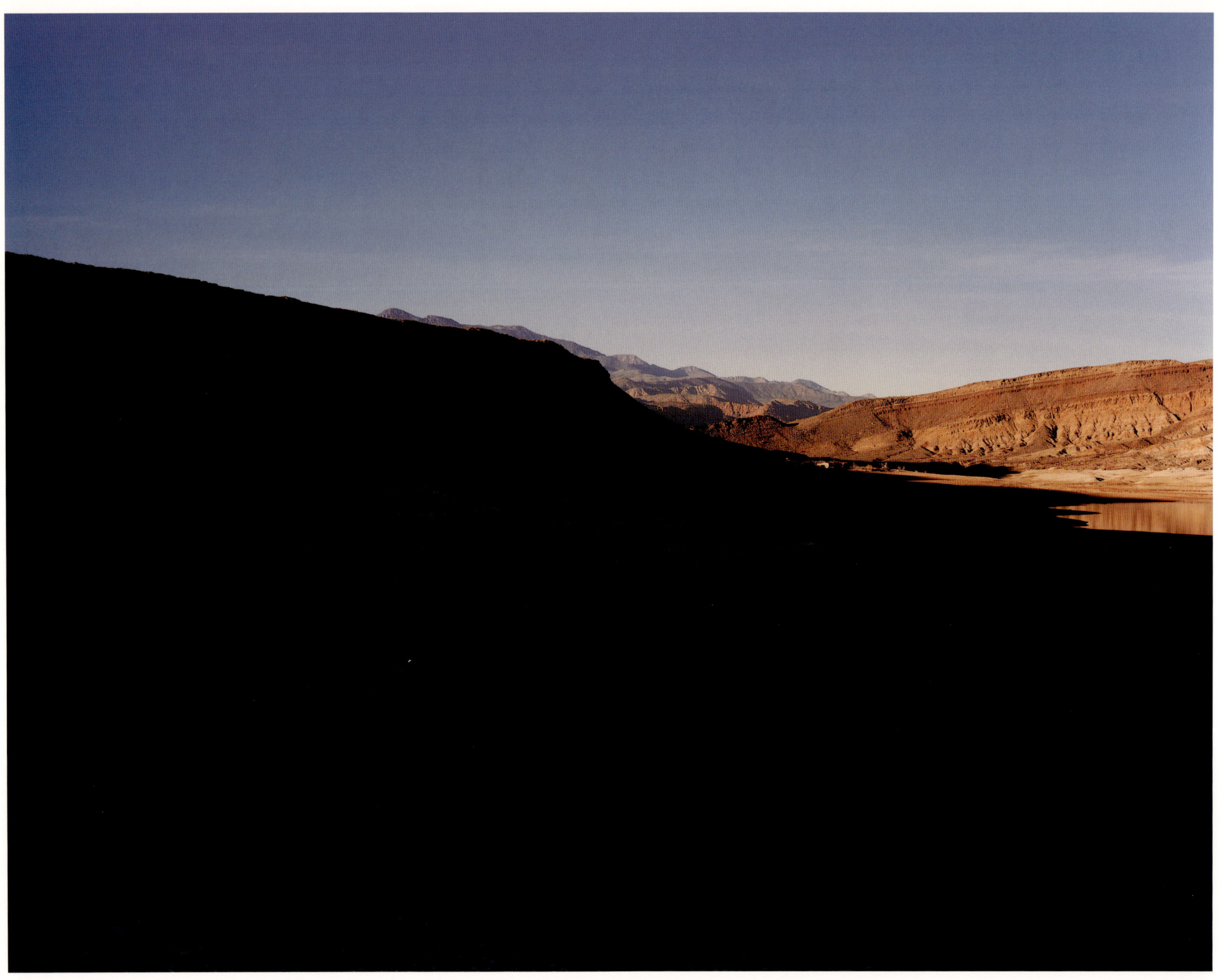

27 | **Reservoir Construction,** Quail Lake, Utah, 2003

28 | **Hoover Dam,** Nevada, 2000

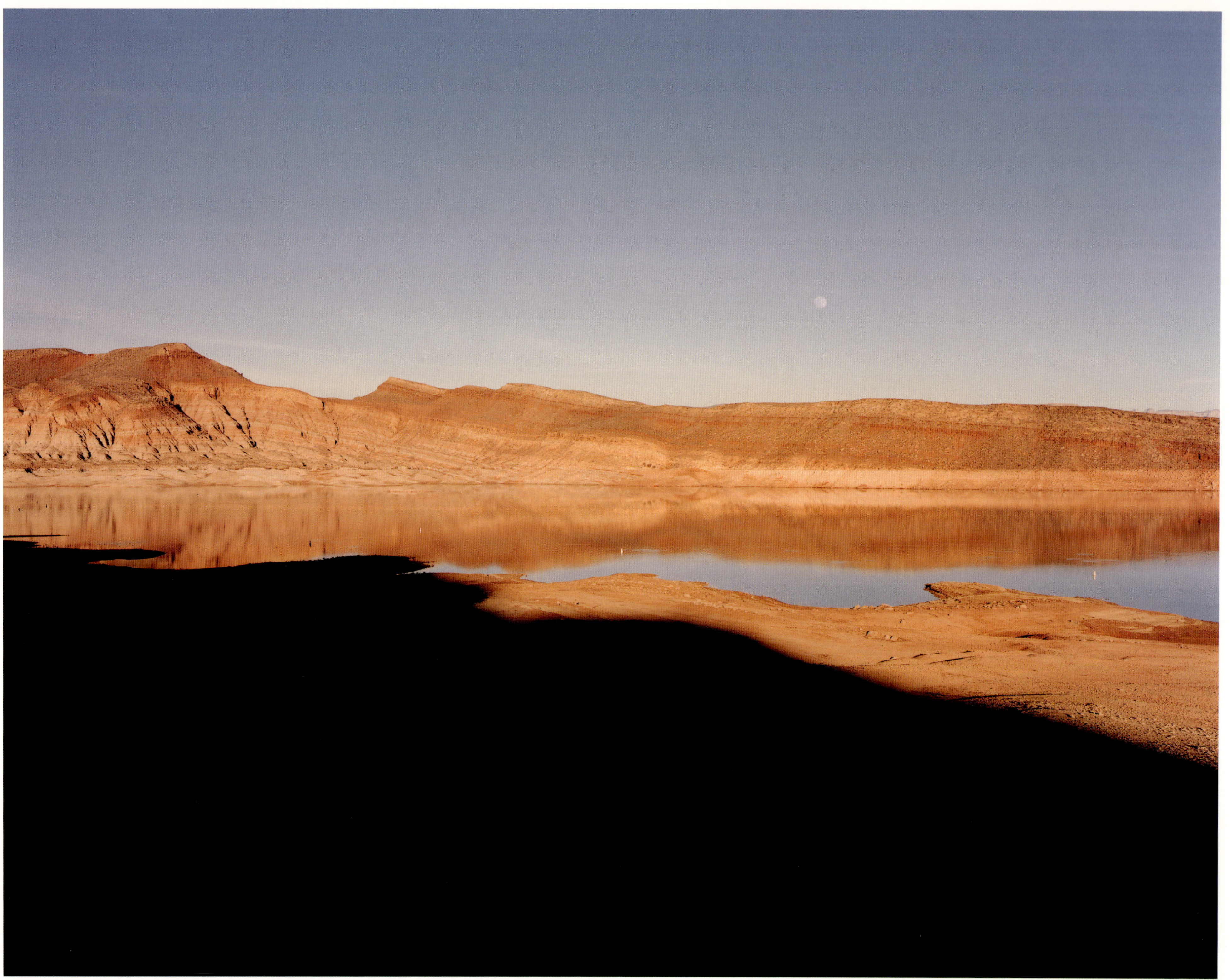

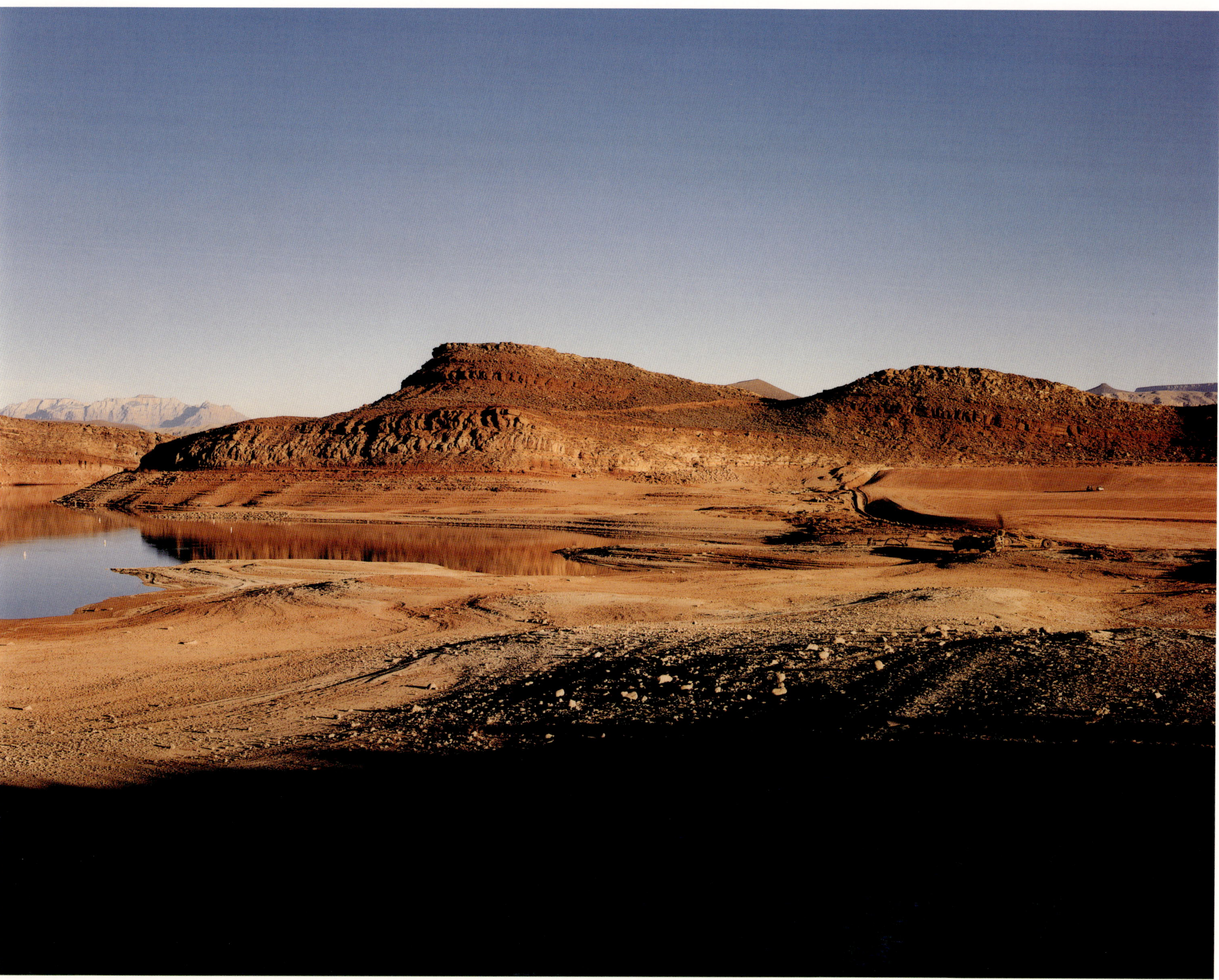

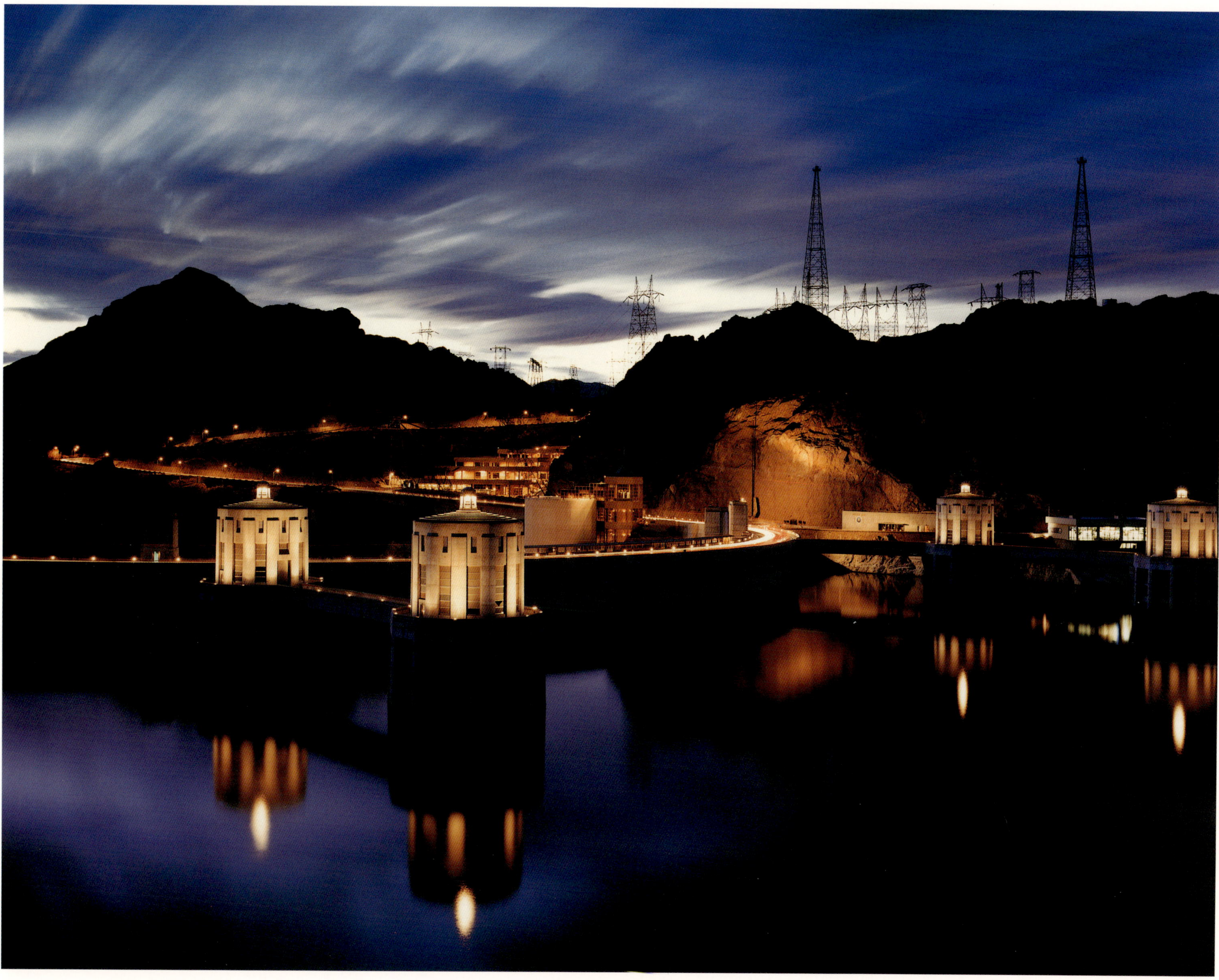

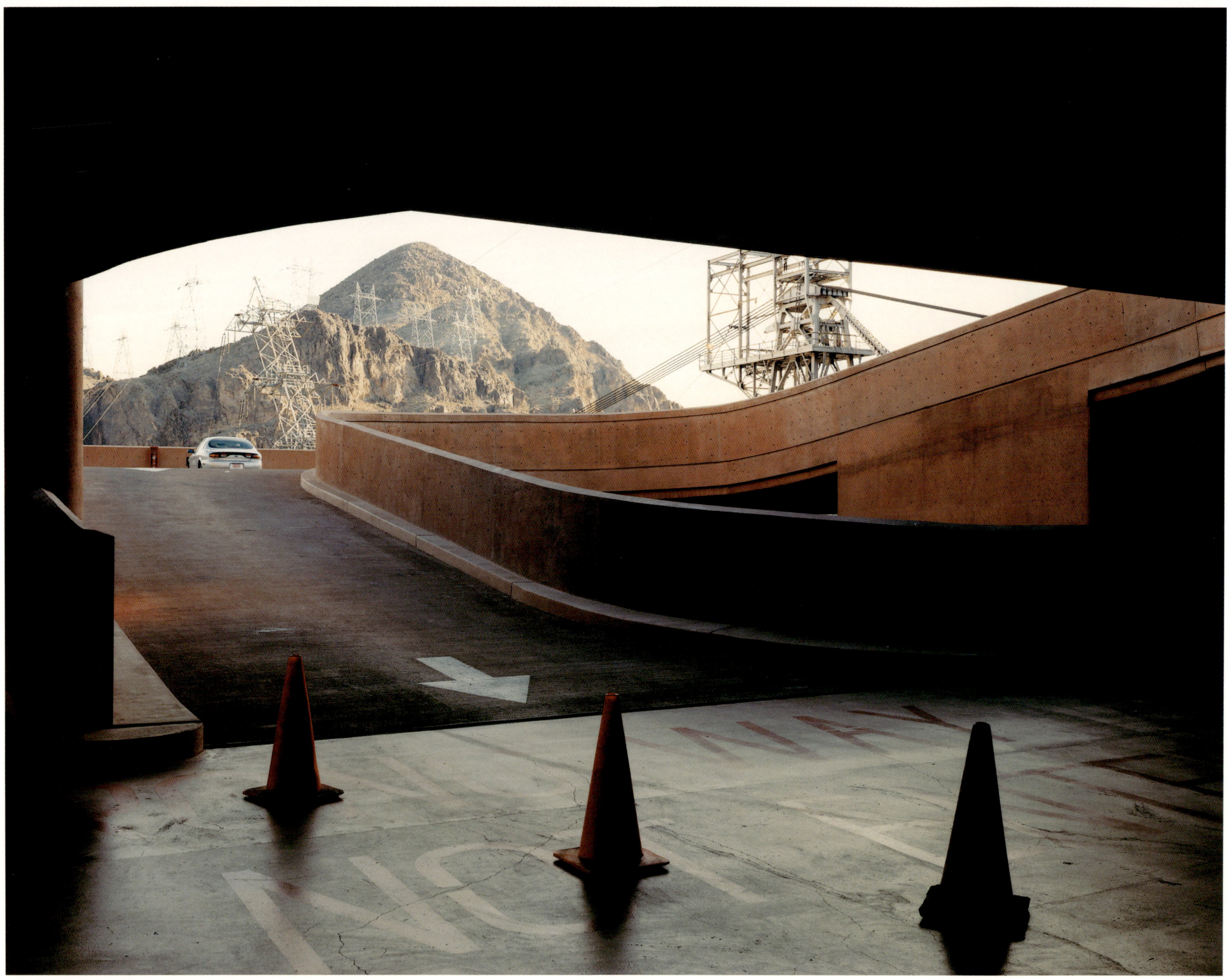

29 | **Parking Garage,** Hoover Dam, Nevada, 1995

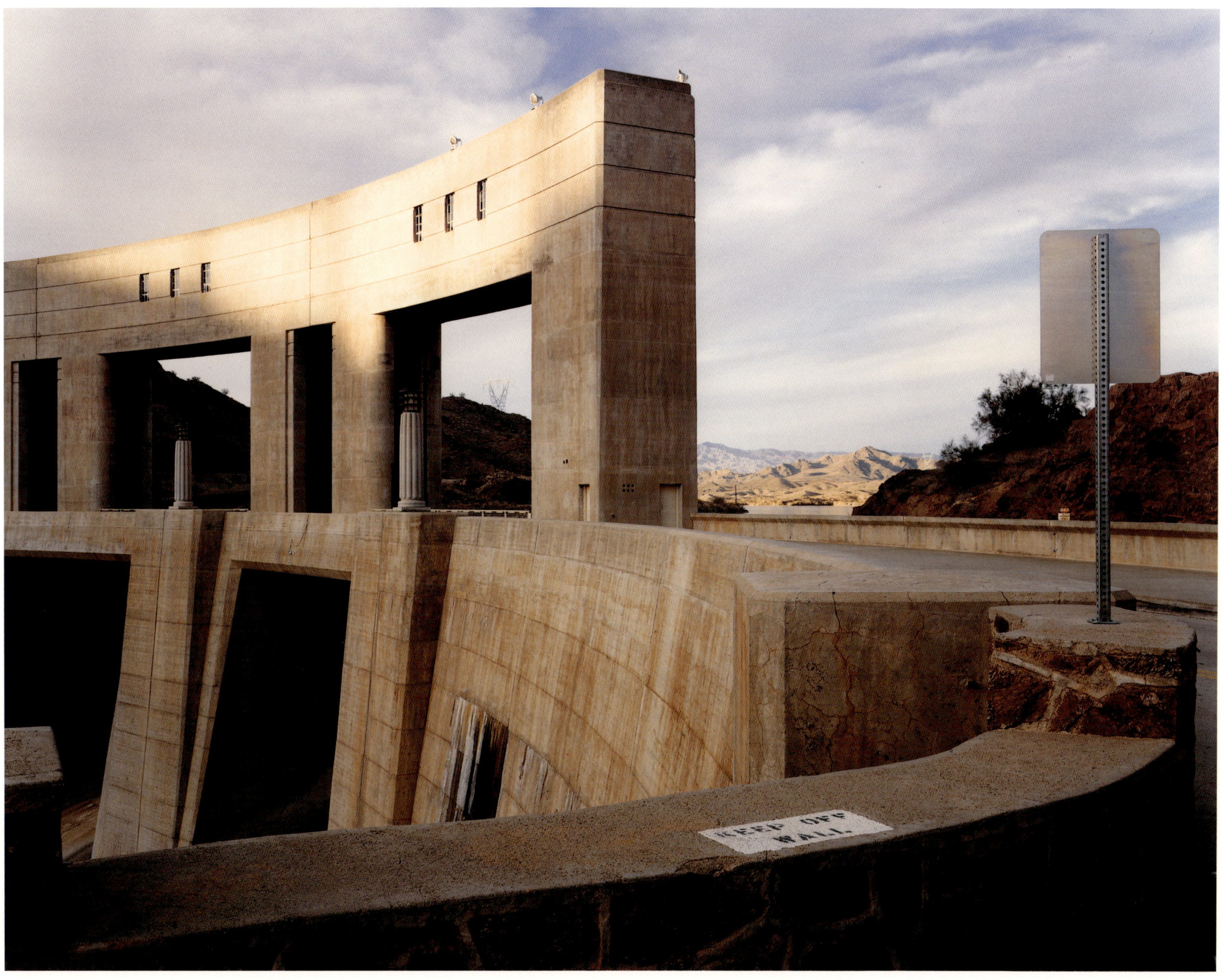

 | **Parker Dam,** Arizona/California, 2002

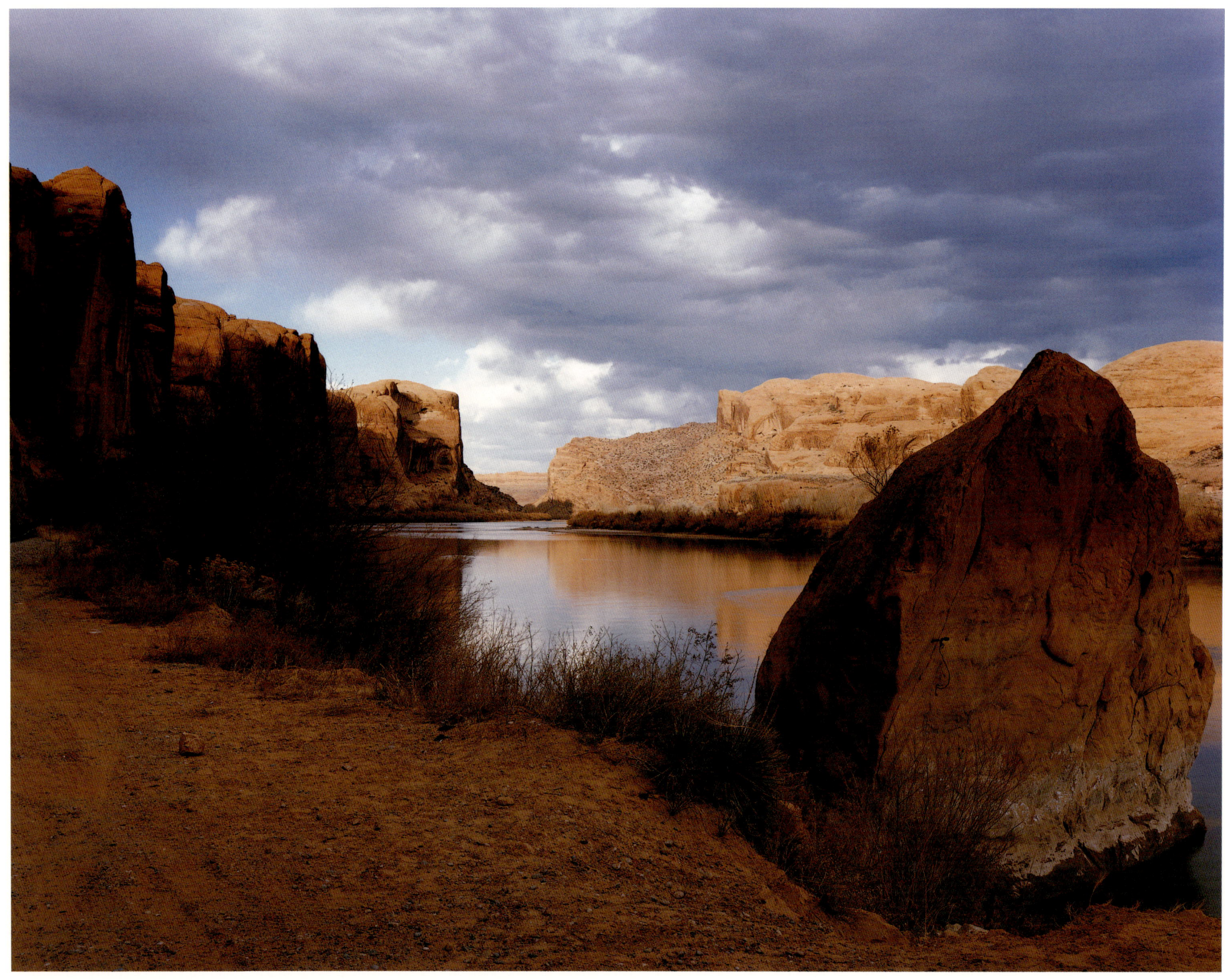

31 | **Colorado River,** Utah, 1998

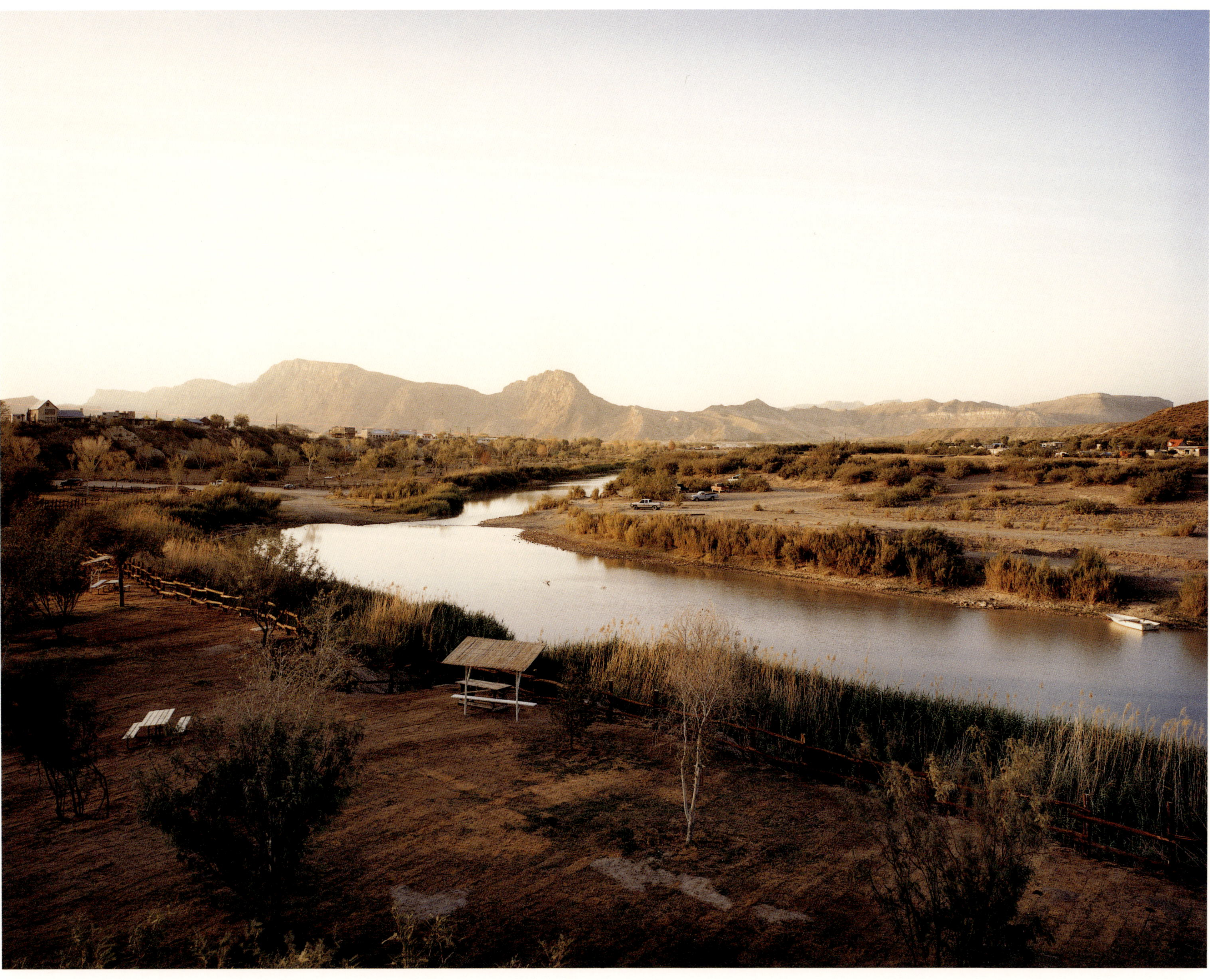

 | **Rio Grande River,** Texas and Mexico, 2001

33 | **Bird Refuge in a Dying Sea,** Salton Sea, California, 1999

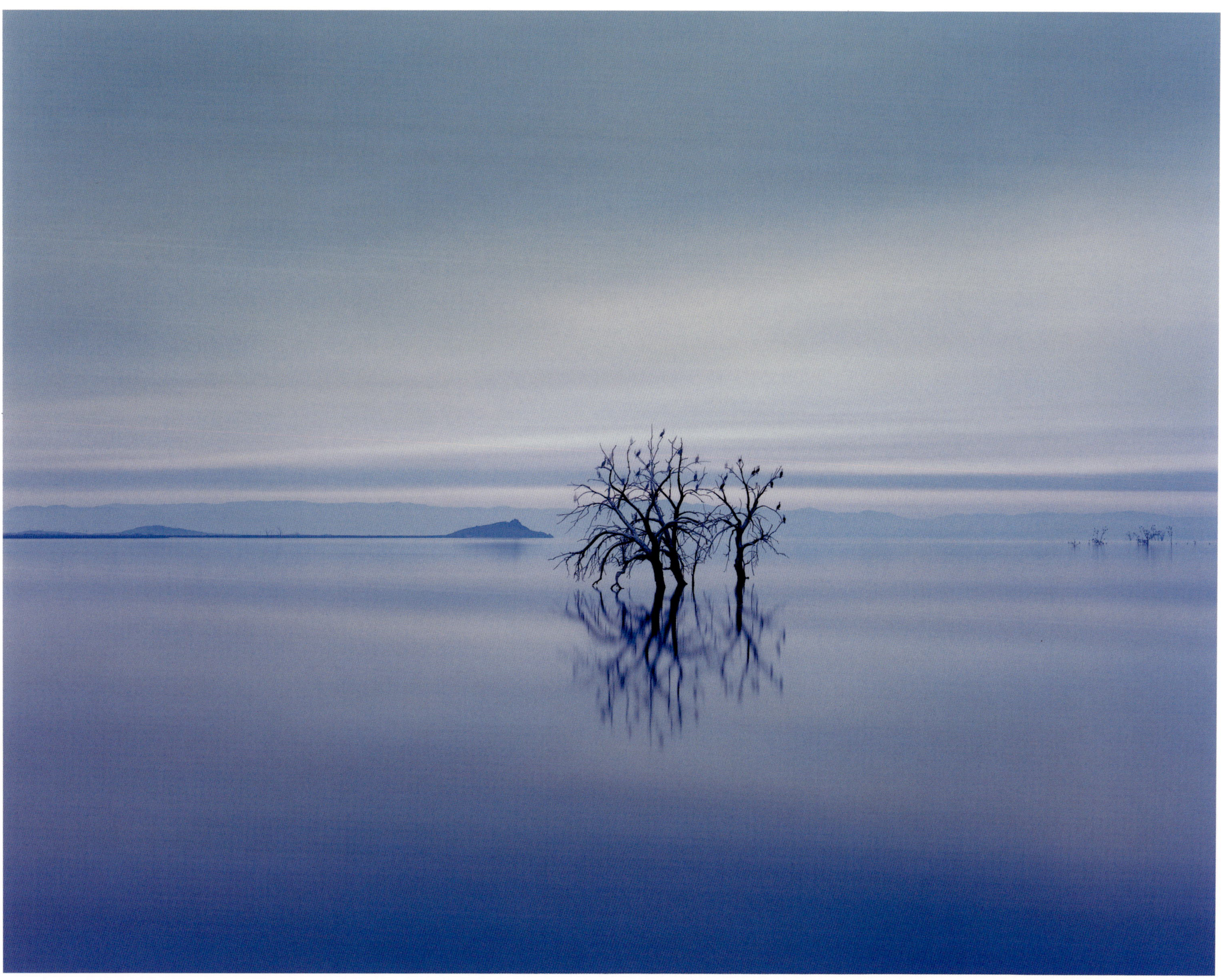

34 | **Desert Oasis: Blue Point Spring,** Nevada, 1997

Sign posted at spring: "Warning, Do Not Allow Water To Enter Your Nose, naegleria fowleri, an amoeba common to thermal pools may enter causing a rare infection and death."

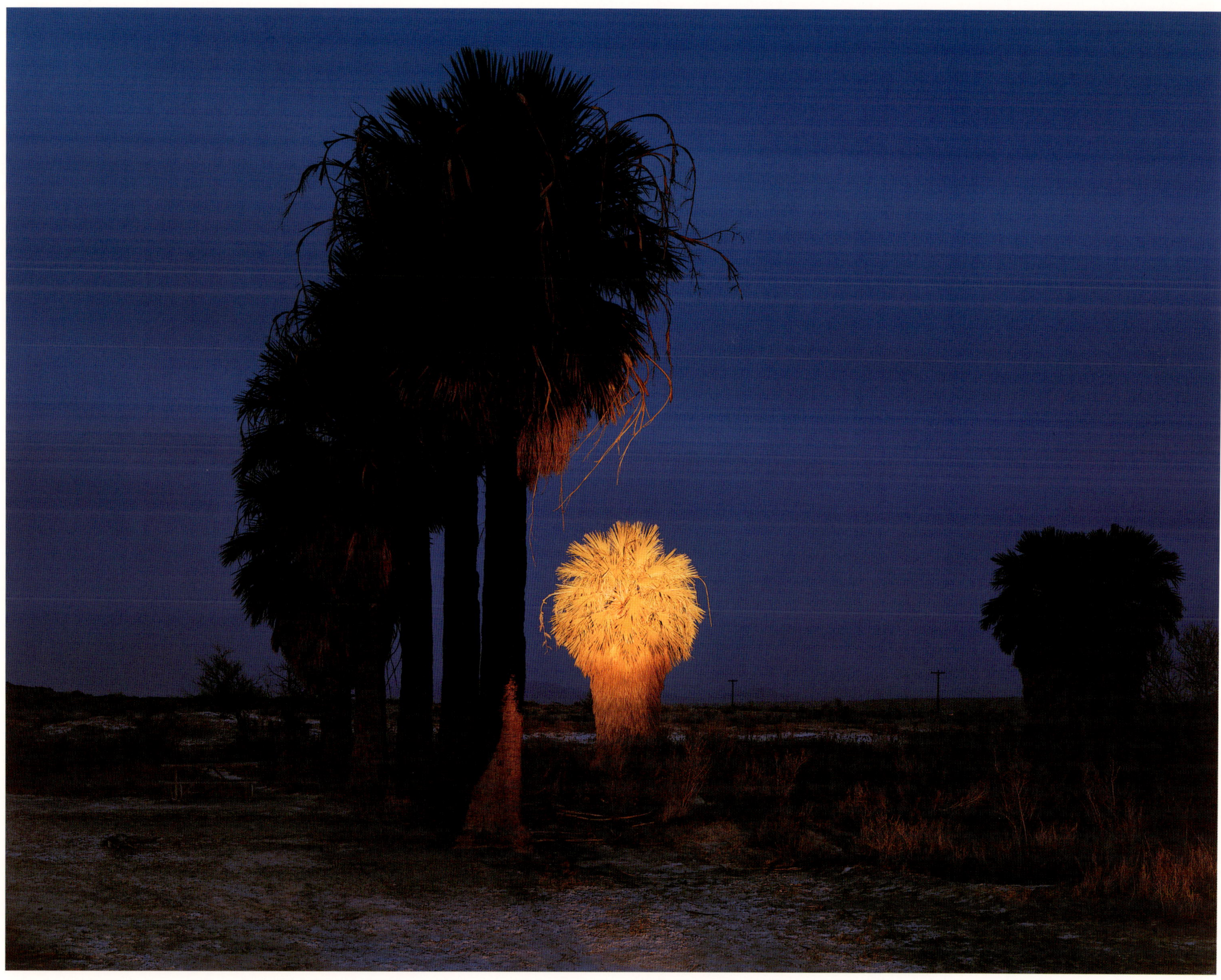

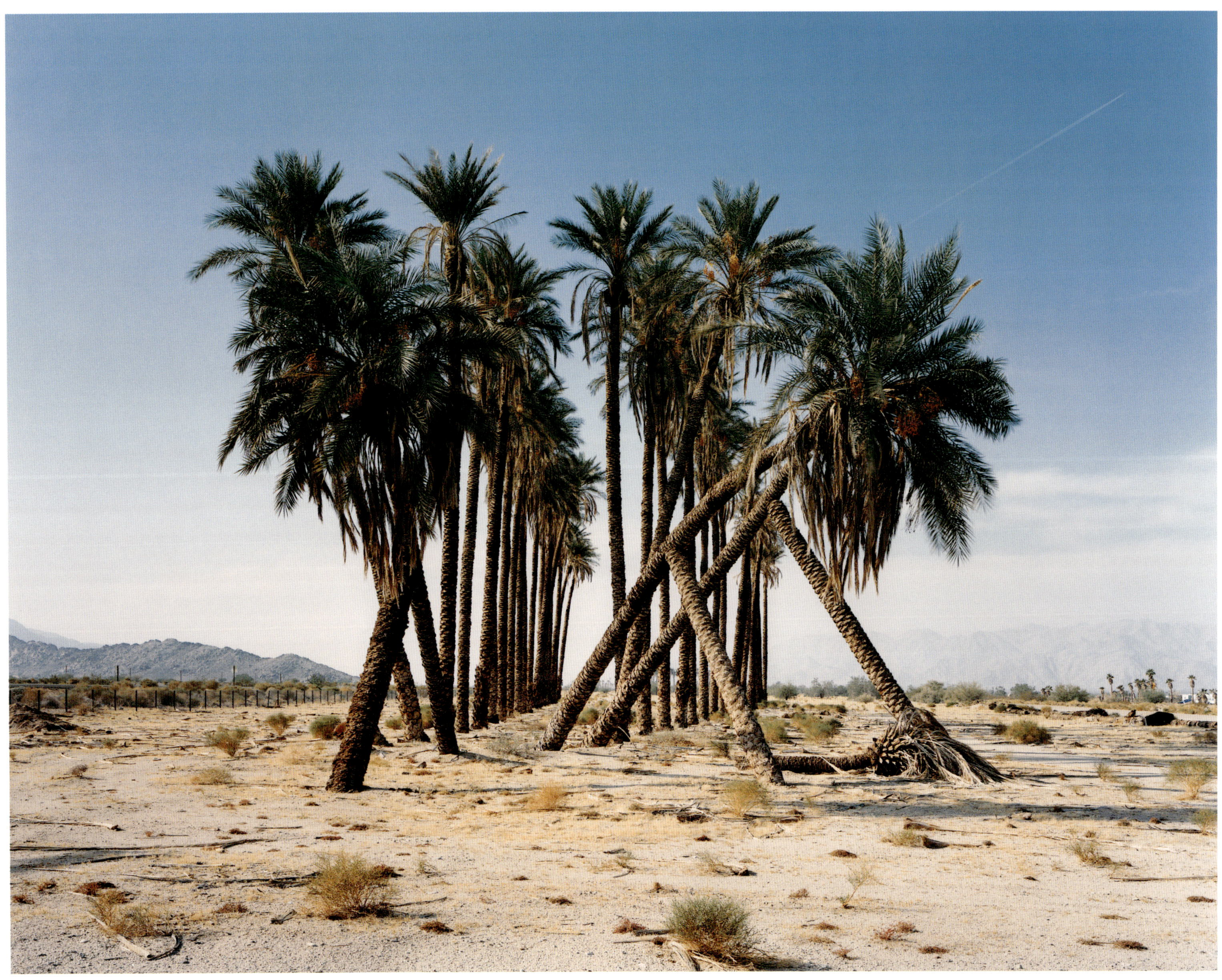

35 | **Desert Center,** California, 2000

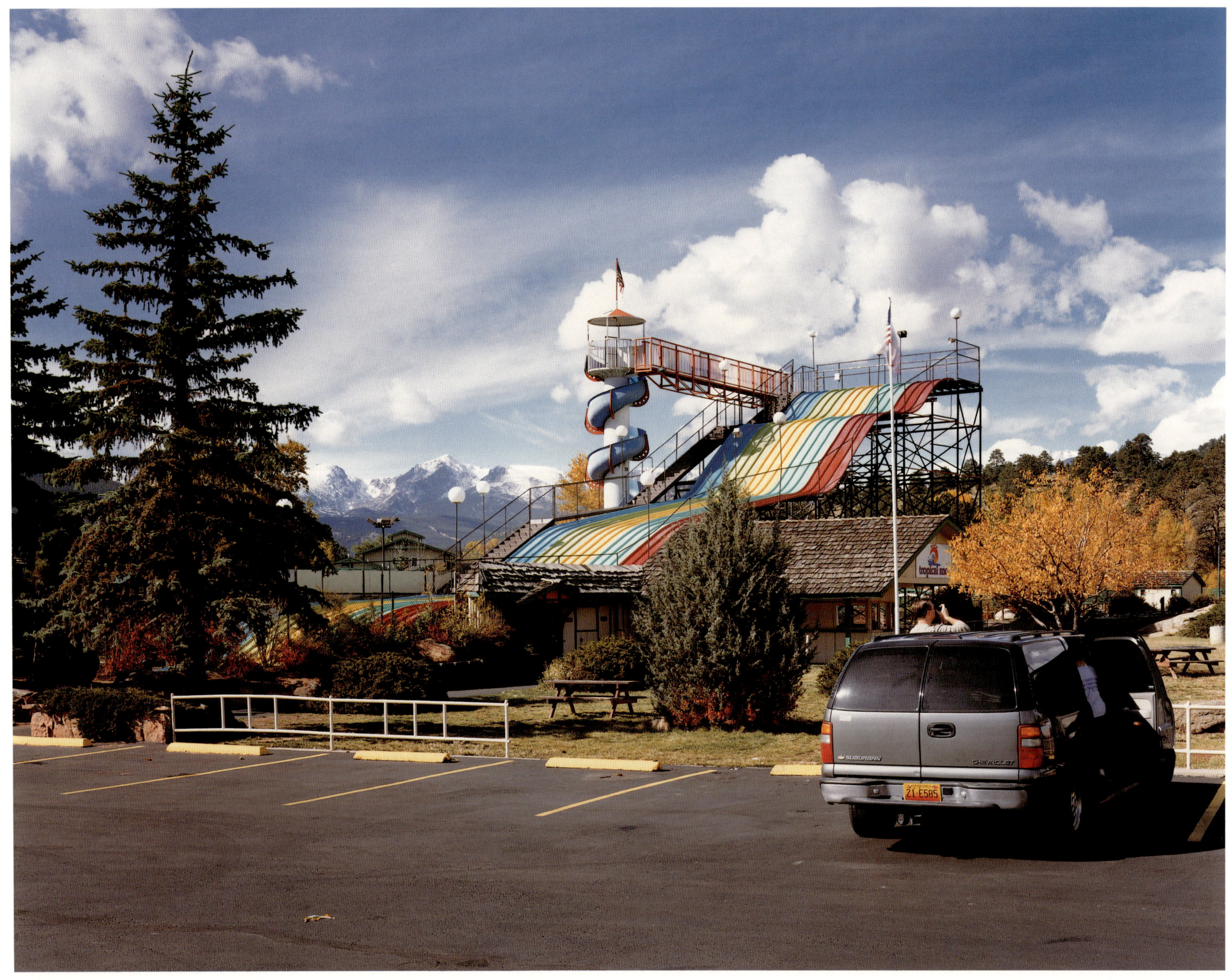

 | **Fun City,** Estes Park, Colorado, 2004

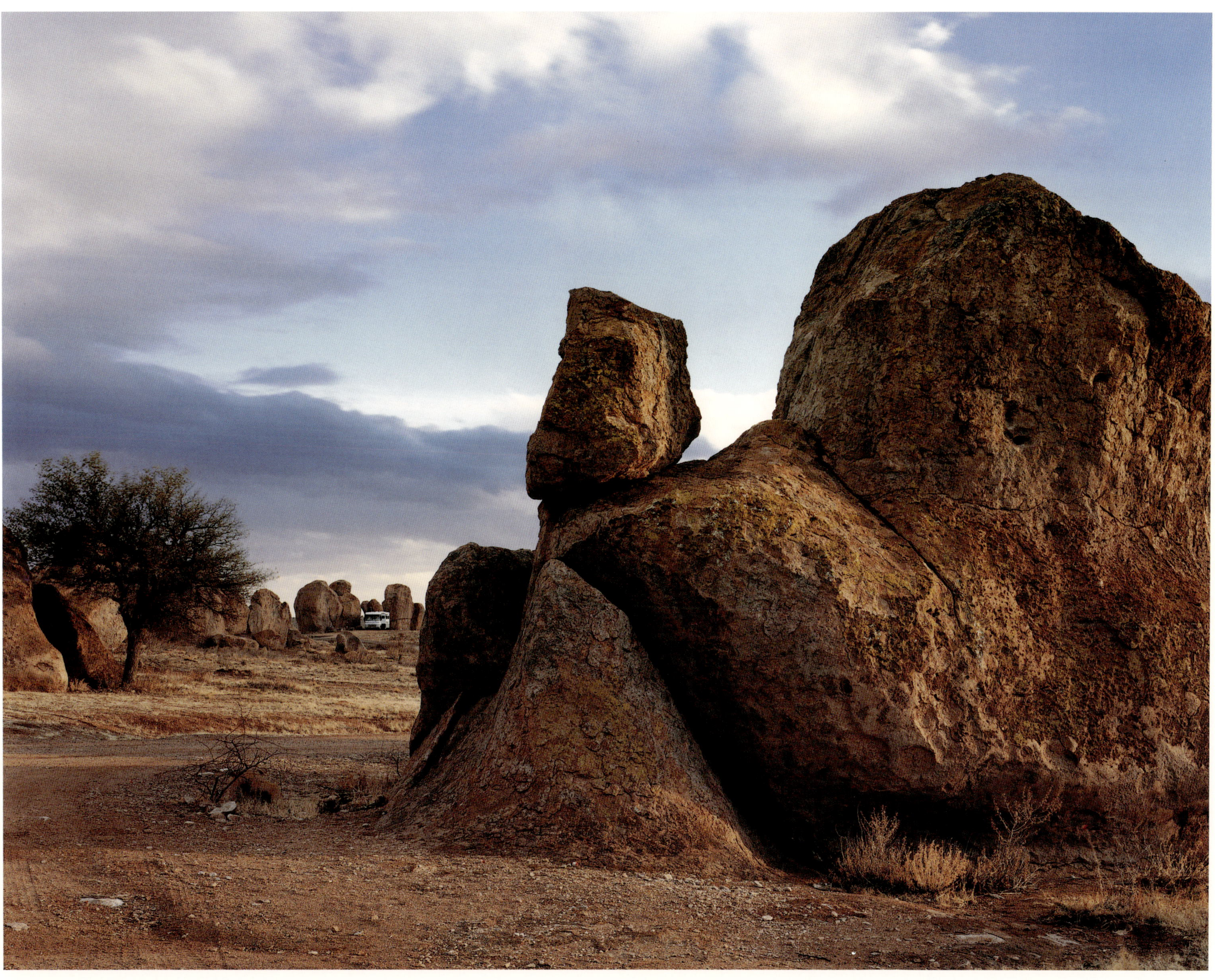

37 | **City of Rocks State Park,** New Mexico, 2002

38 | **Mitchell Butte,** Utah/Arizona Border, 1995

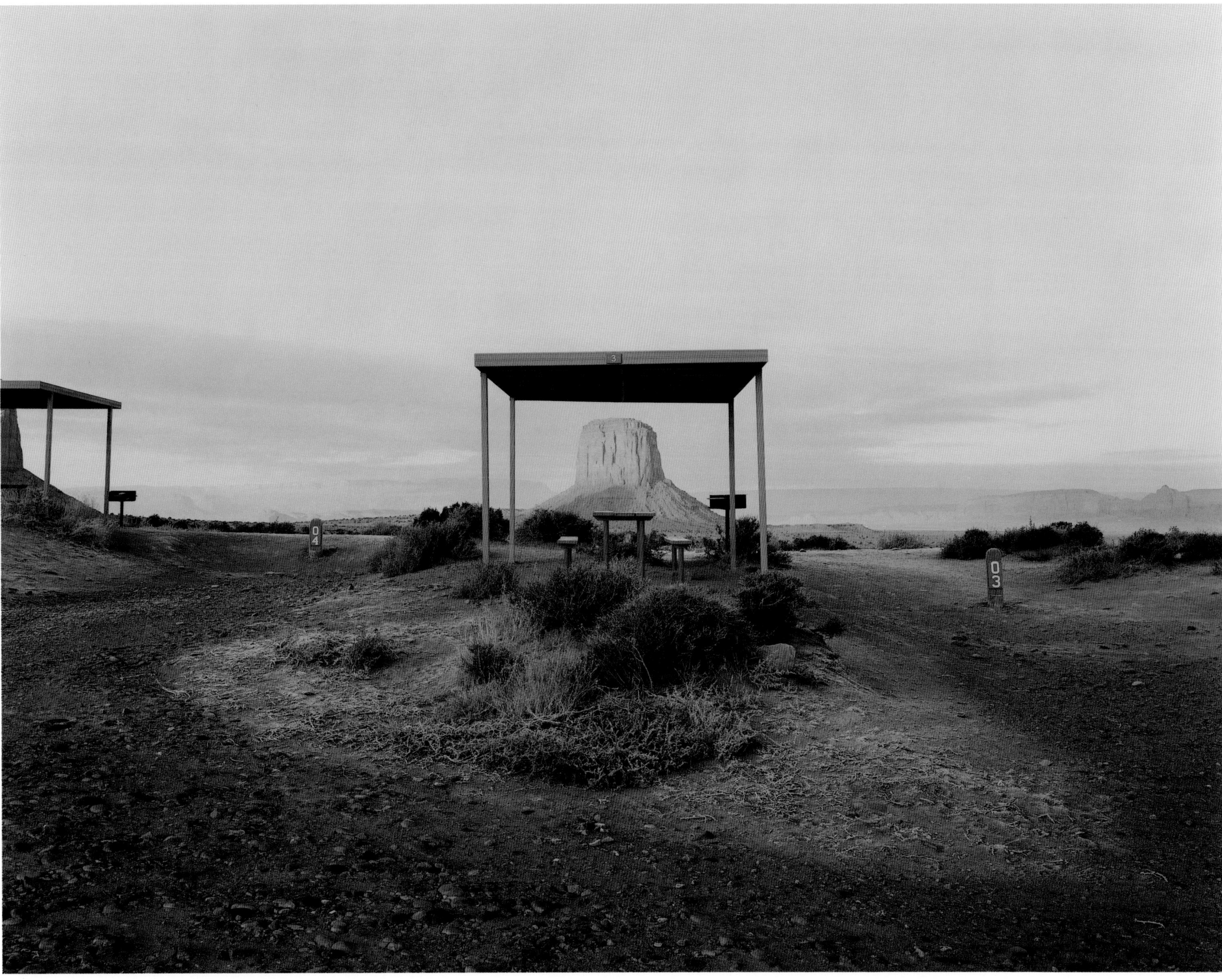
3
04
03

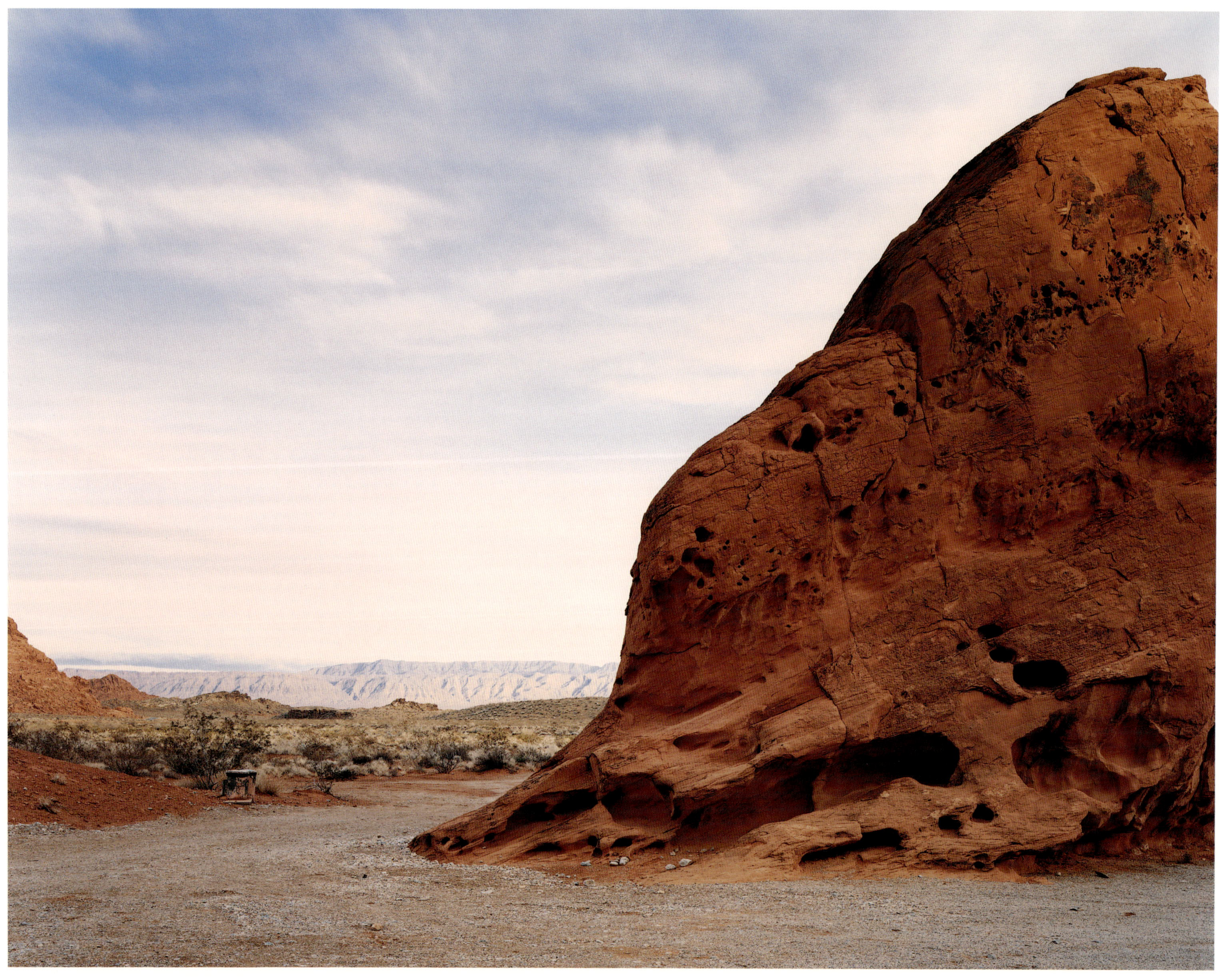

39 | **Valley of Fire State Park,** Nevada, 2003

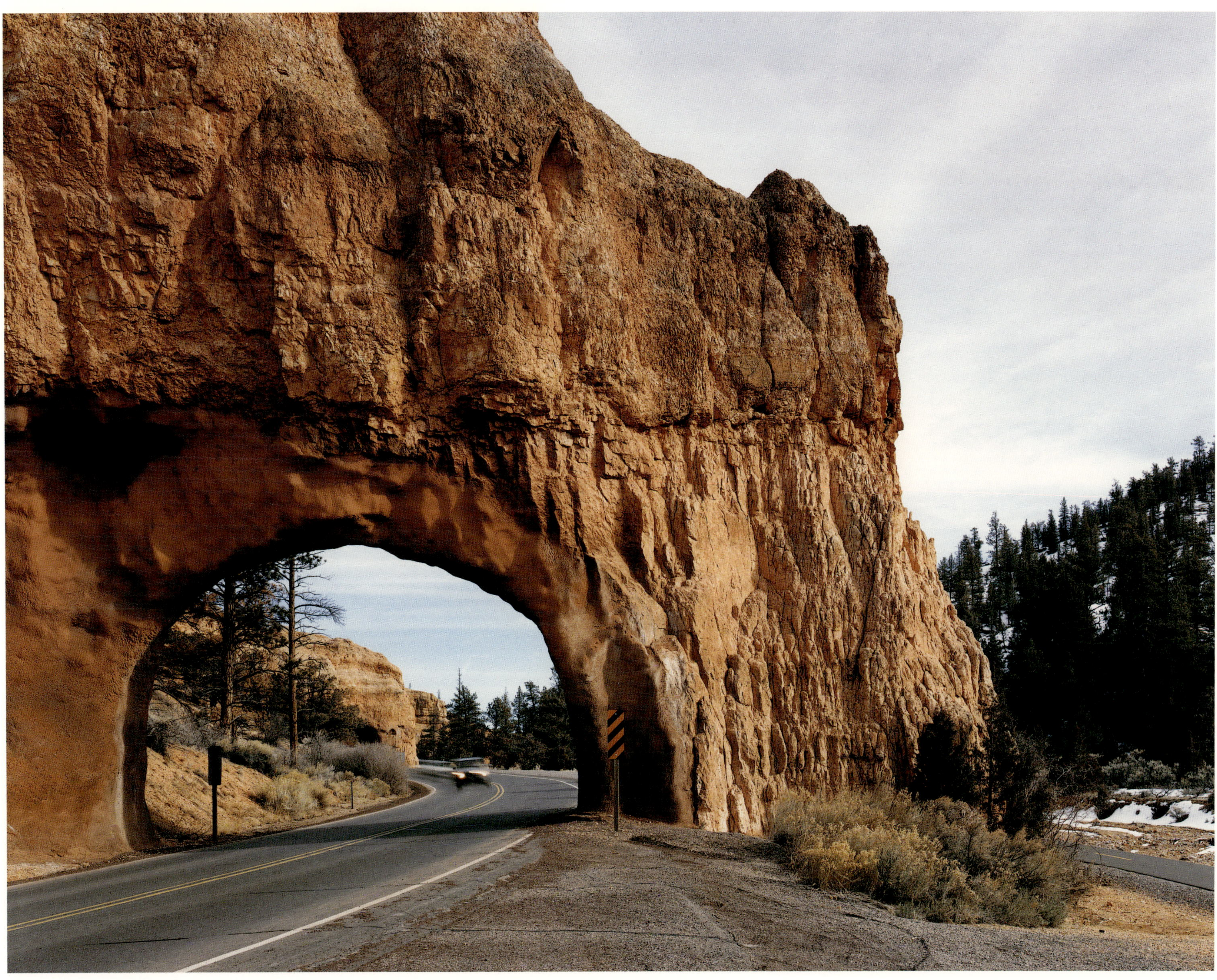

40 | **Manmade Arch,** Red Canyon, Utah, 2003

41 | **Warm Creek Road,** Utah, 1997

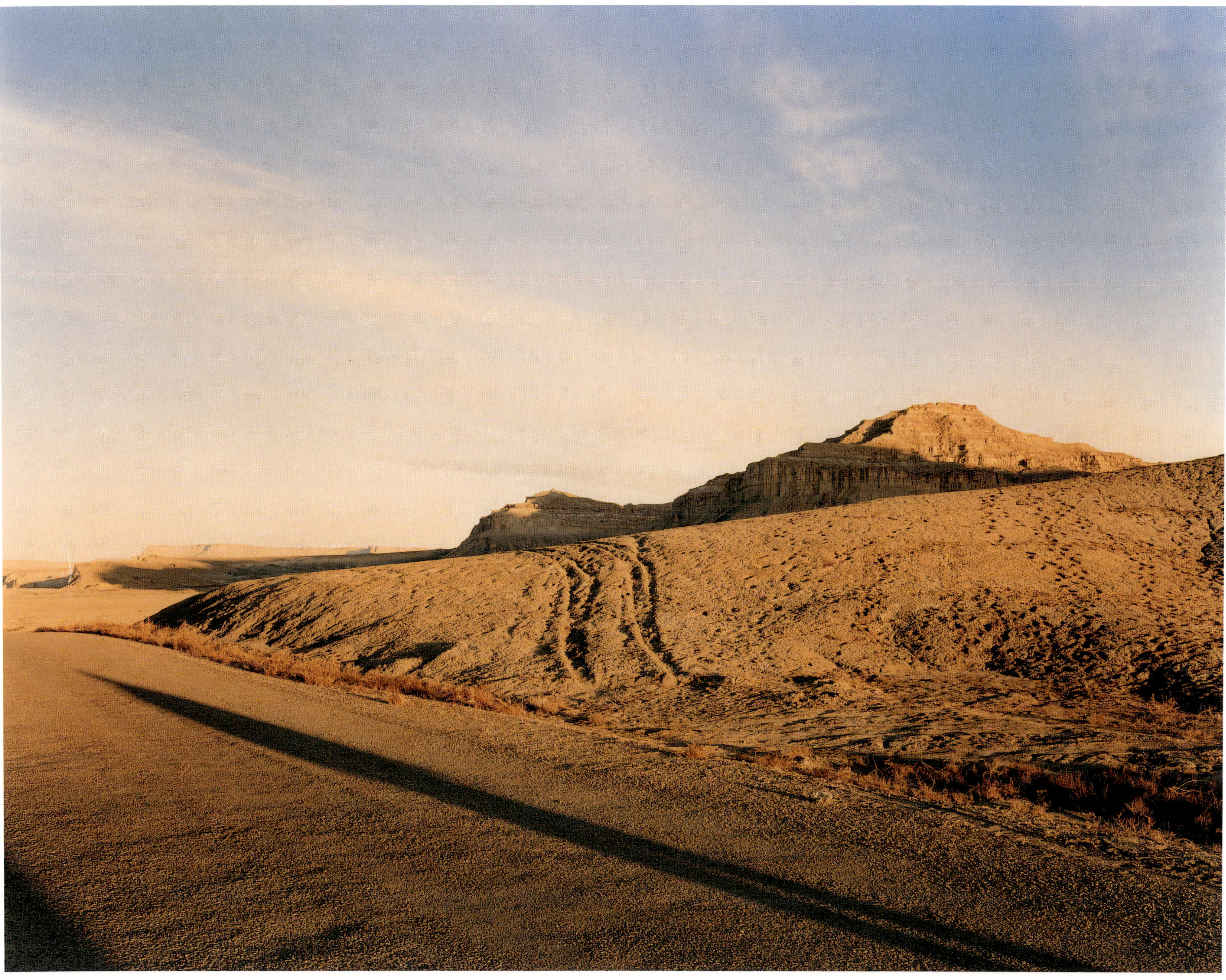

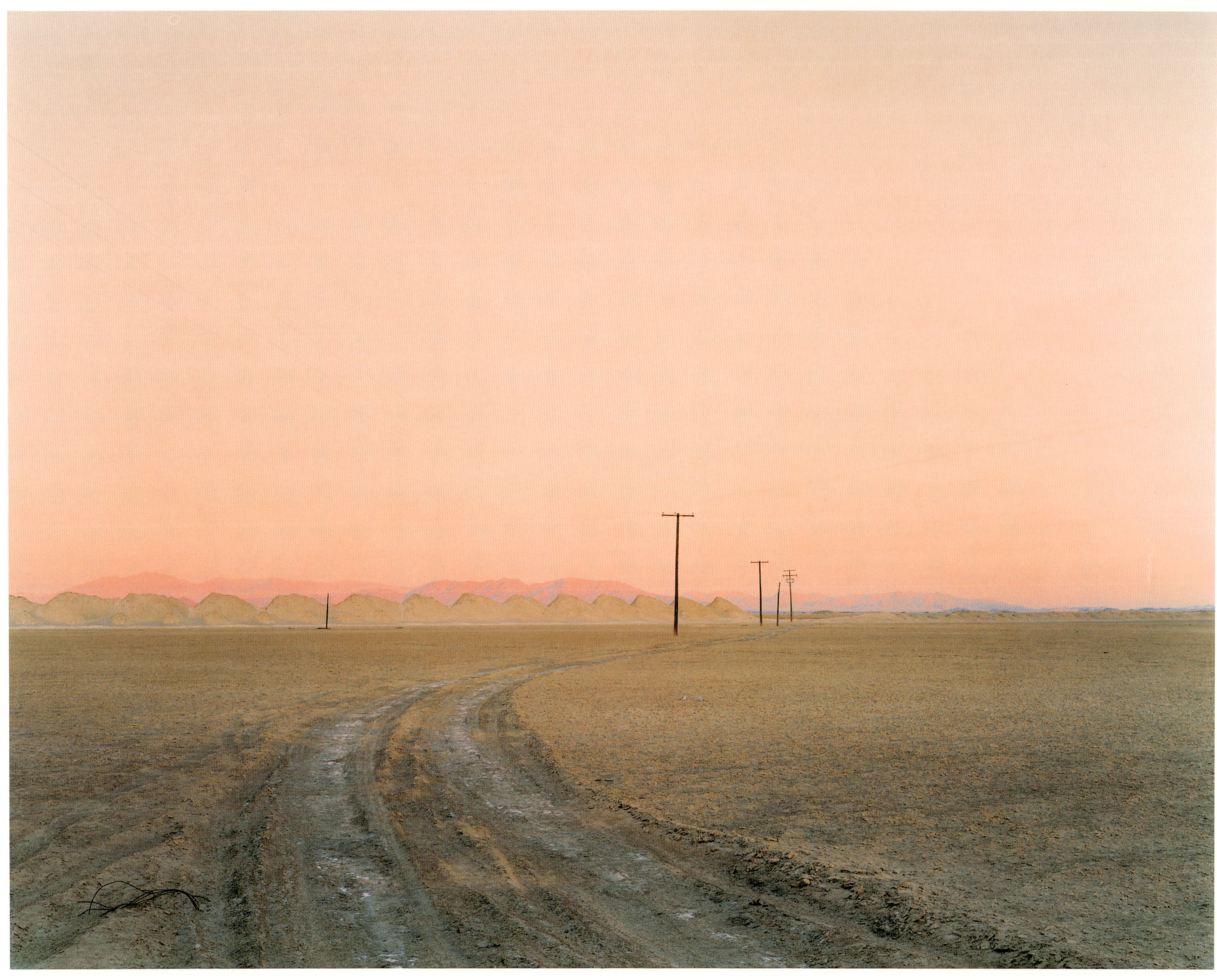

 | **Bristol Dry Lake,** California, 2003

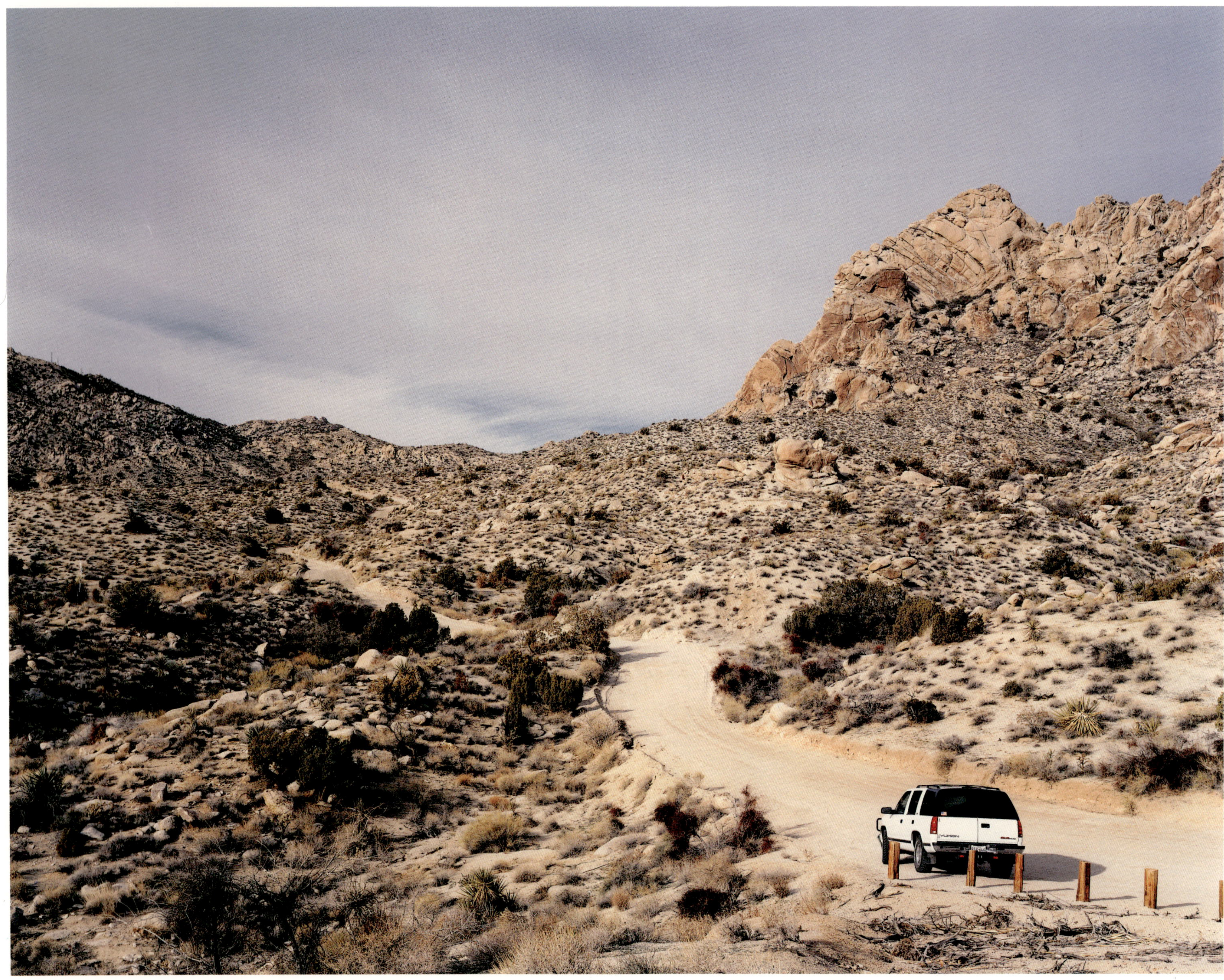

 | **Christmas Tree Pass,** Nevada, 2003

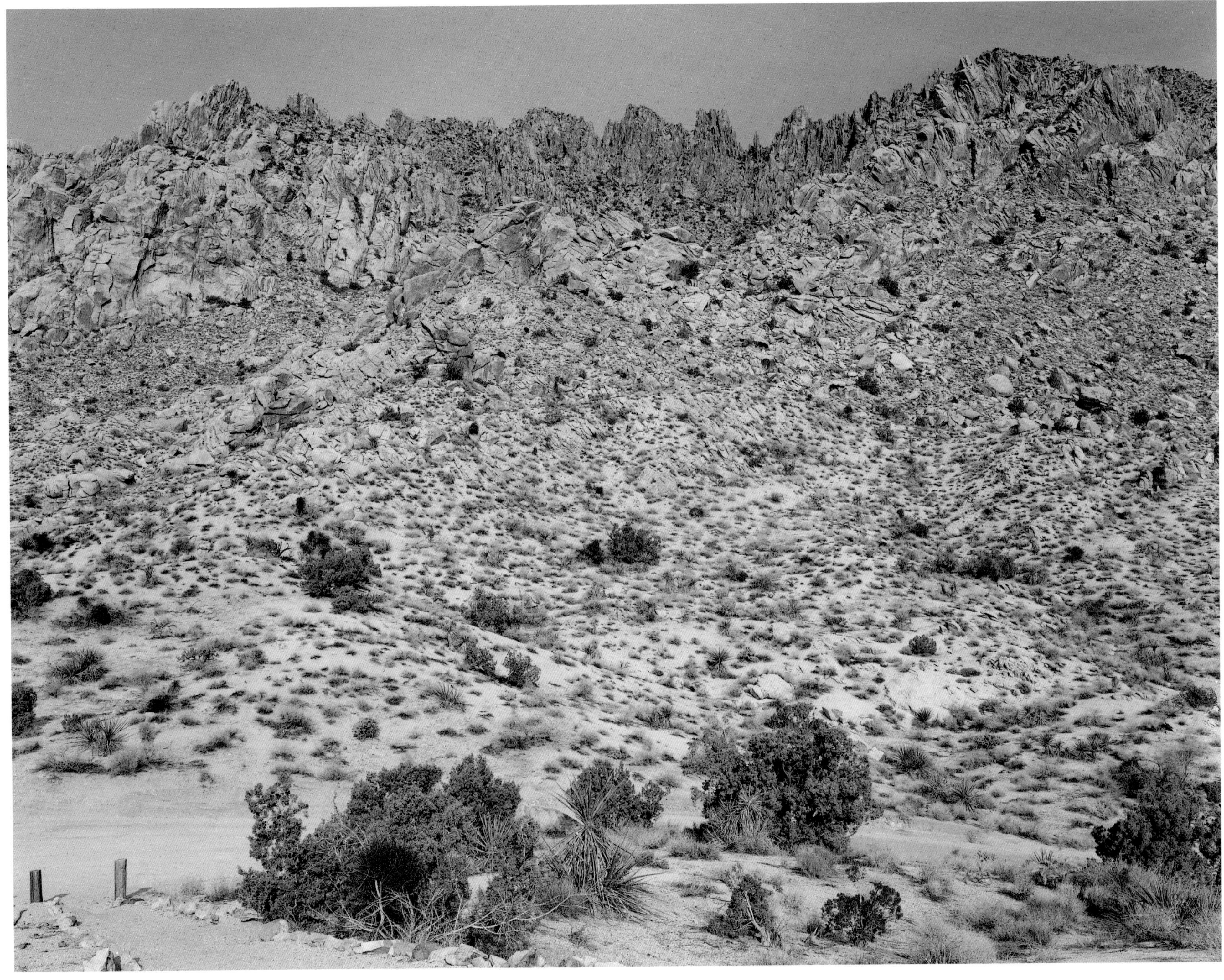

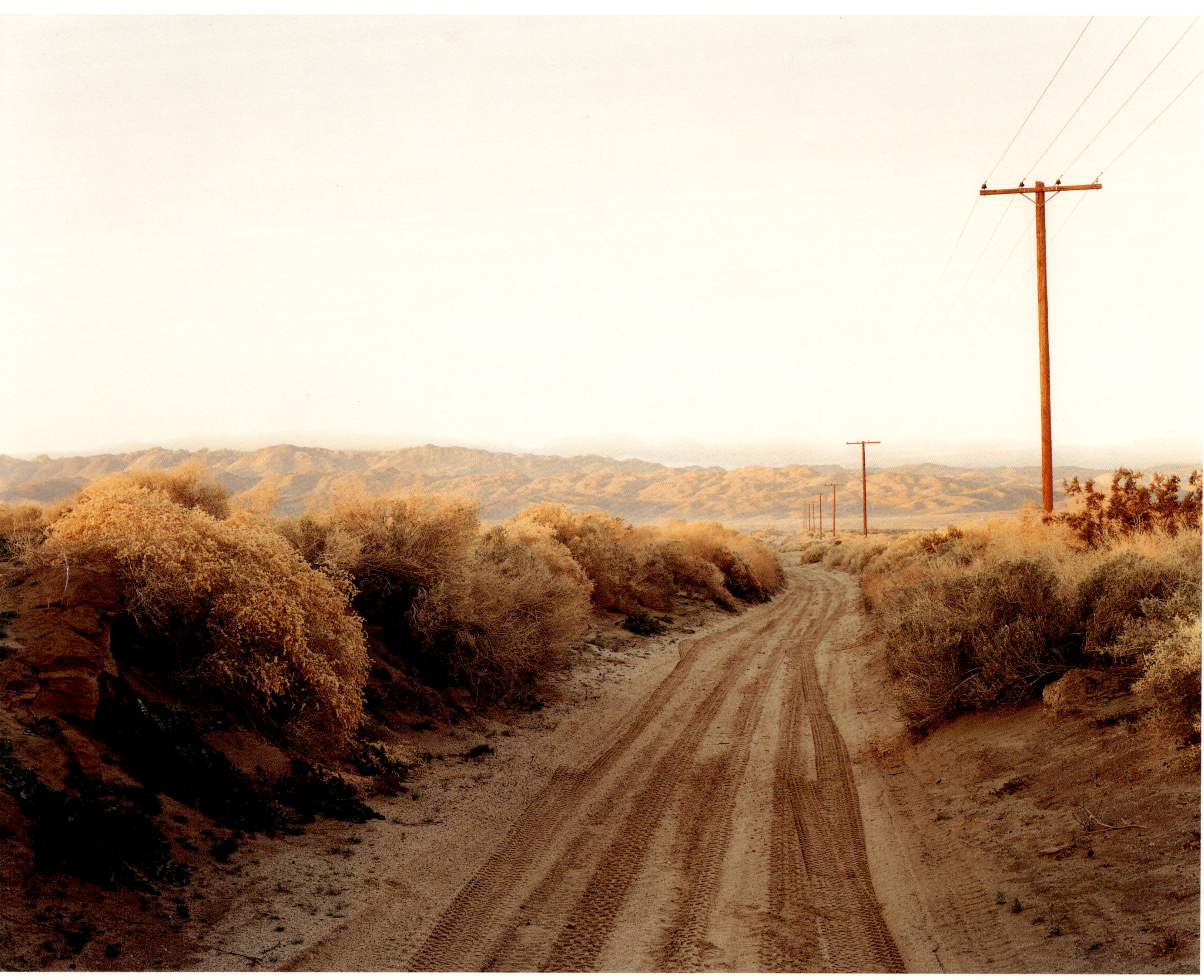

 | **Yuha Desert,** California, 1997

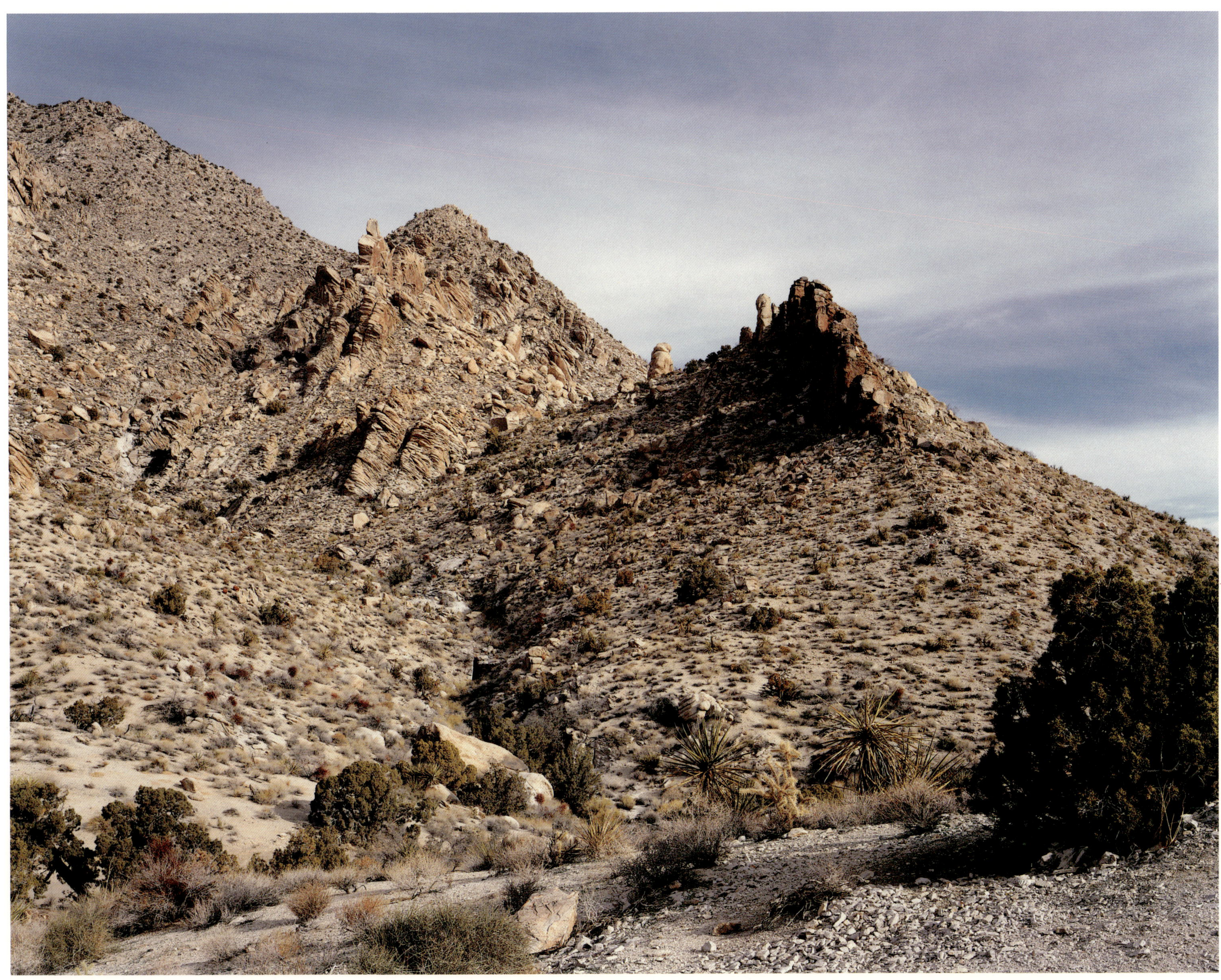

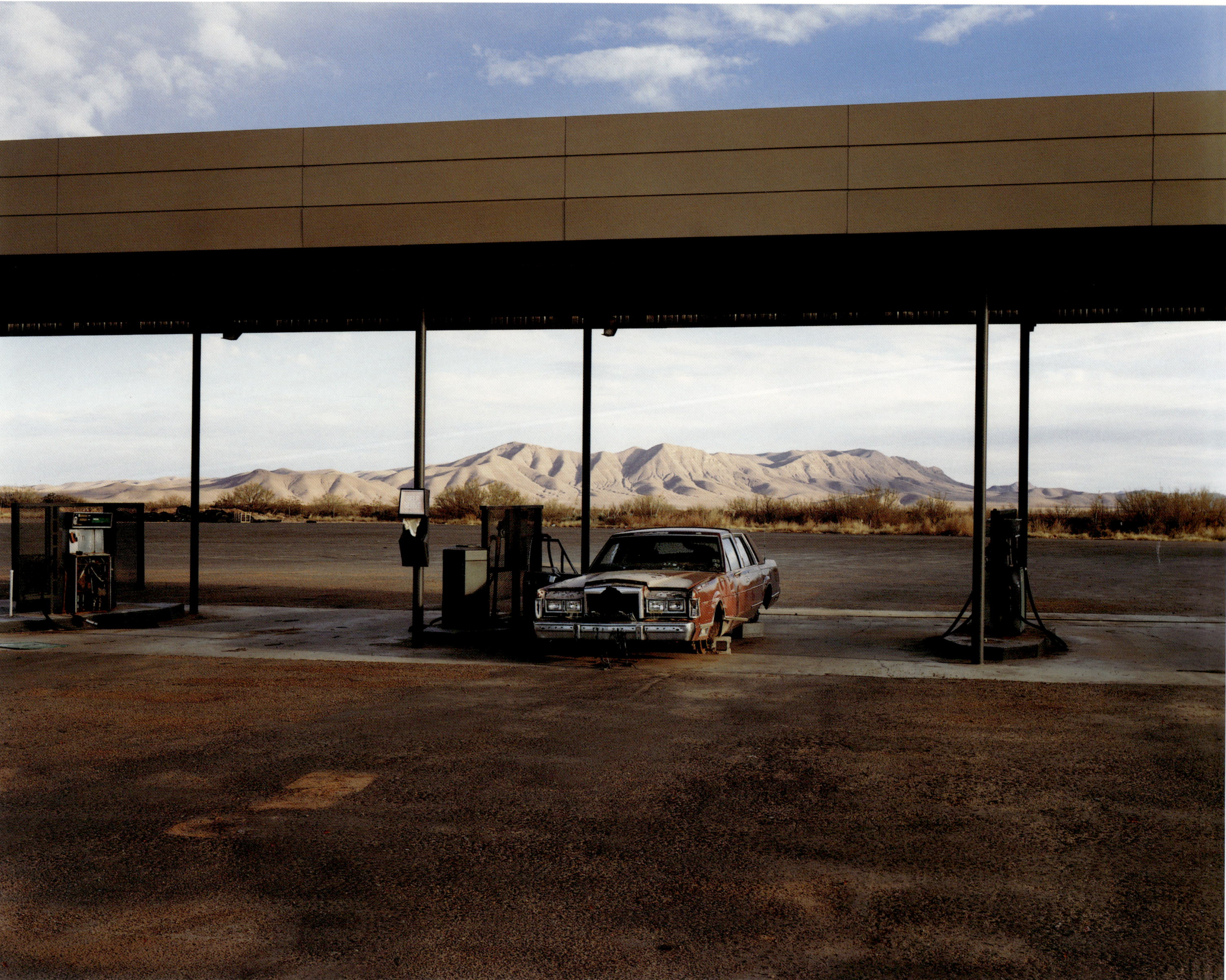

45 | **West Texas,** 2001

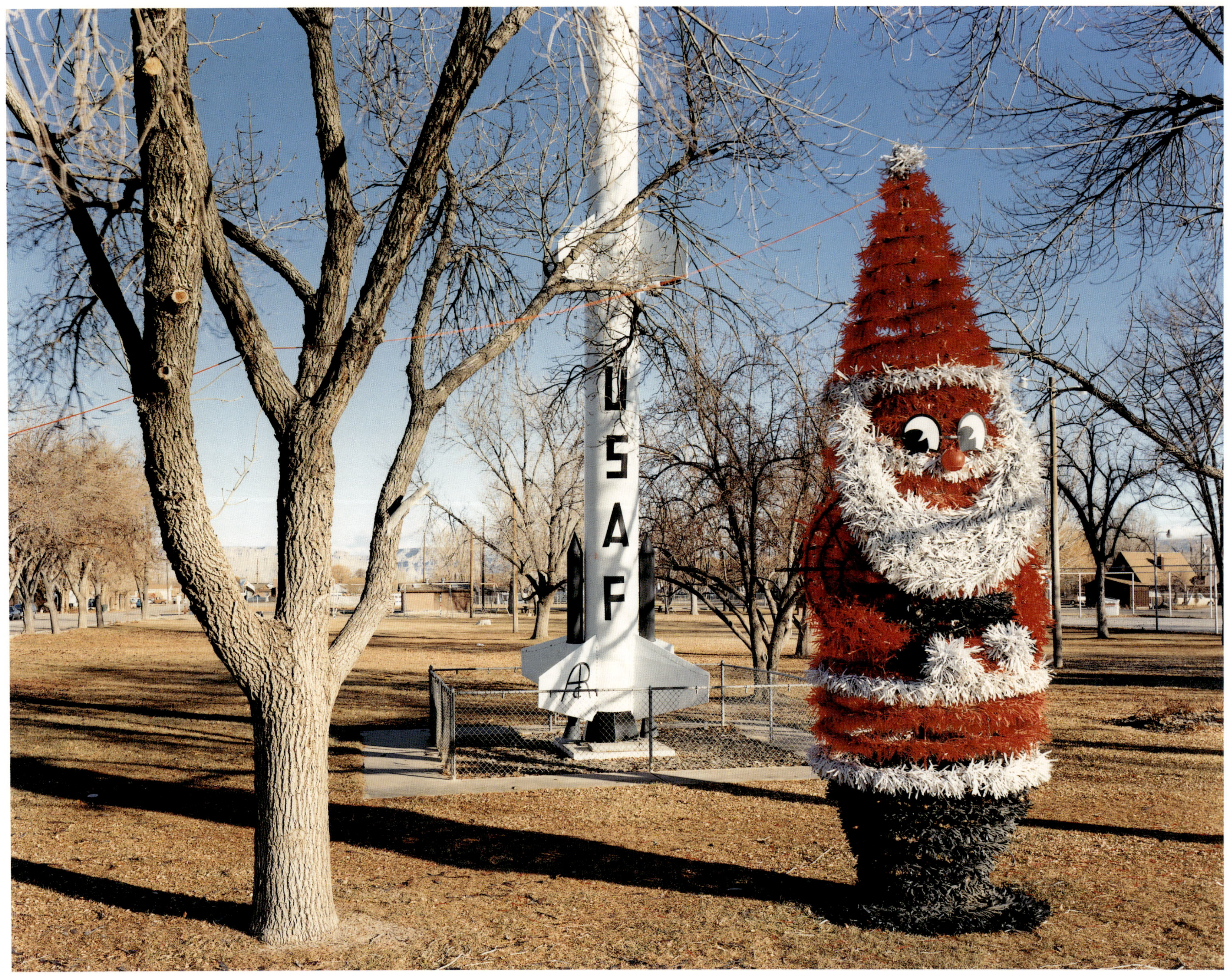

 | **Green River City Park,** Utah, 1997

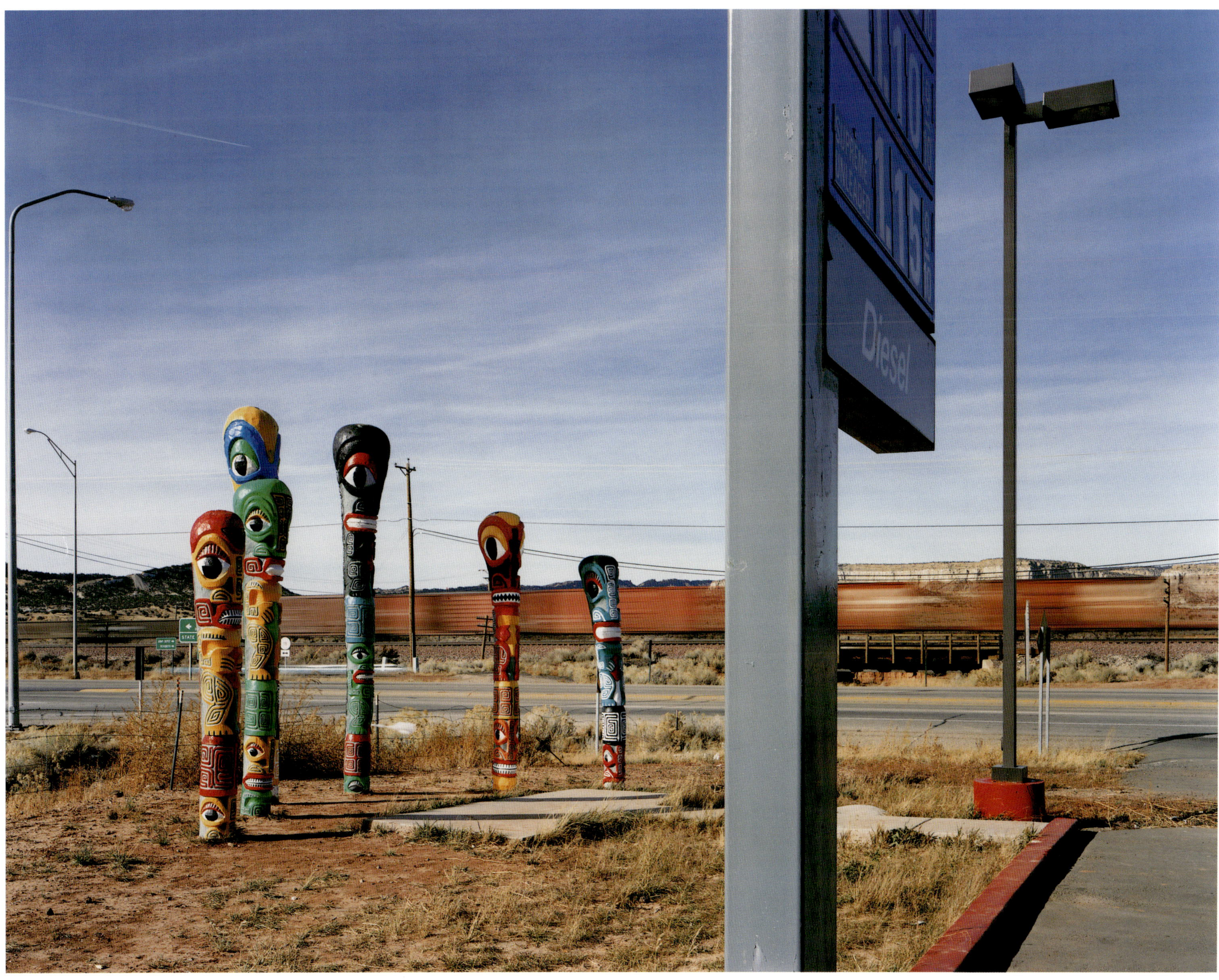

47 | **Gallup, New Mexico,** 1995

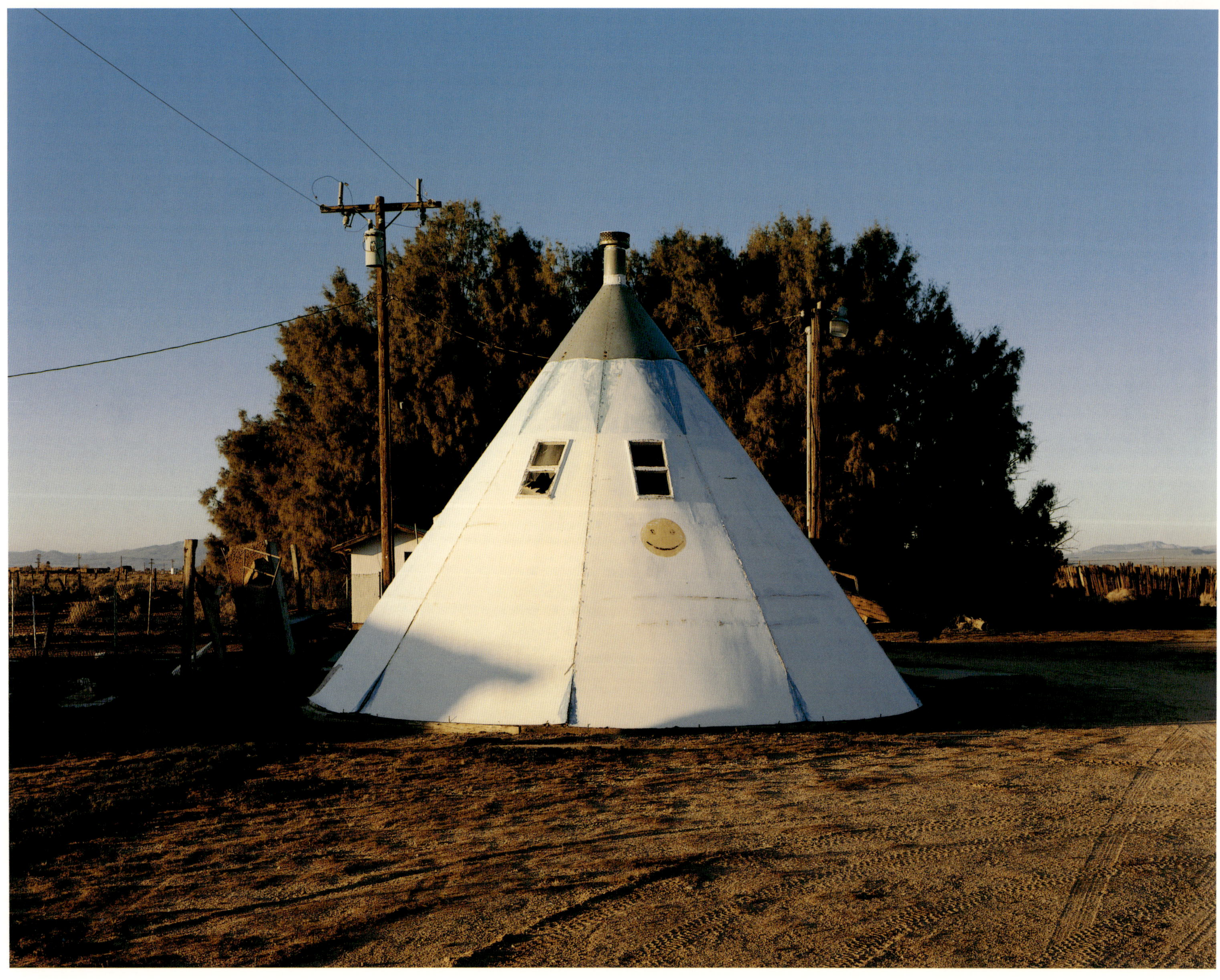

 | **Barstow, California,** 2005

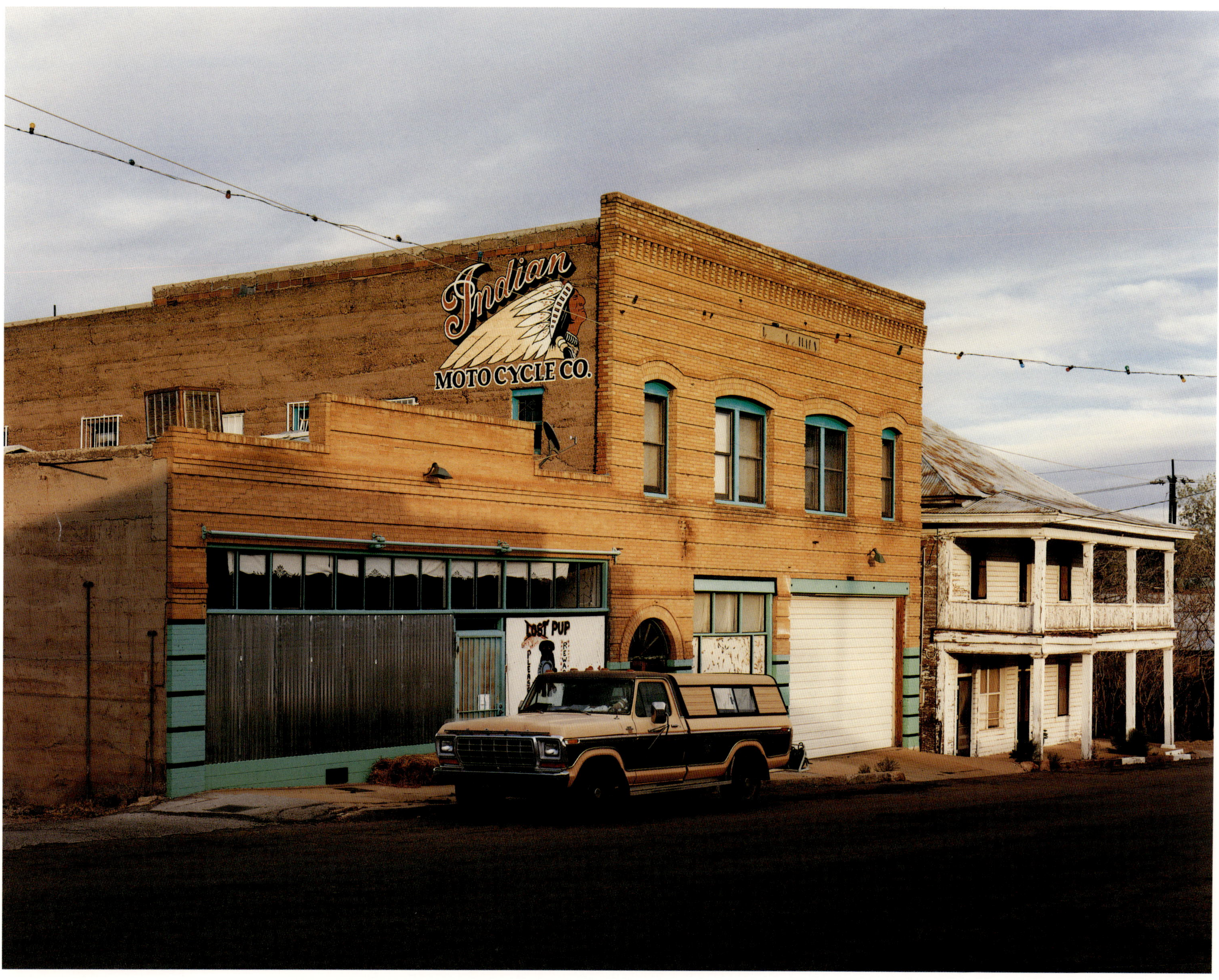

49 | Bisbee, Arizona, 1999

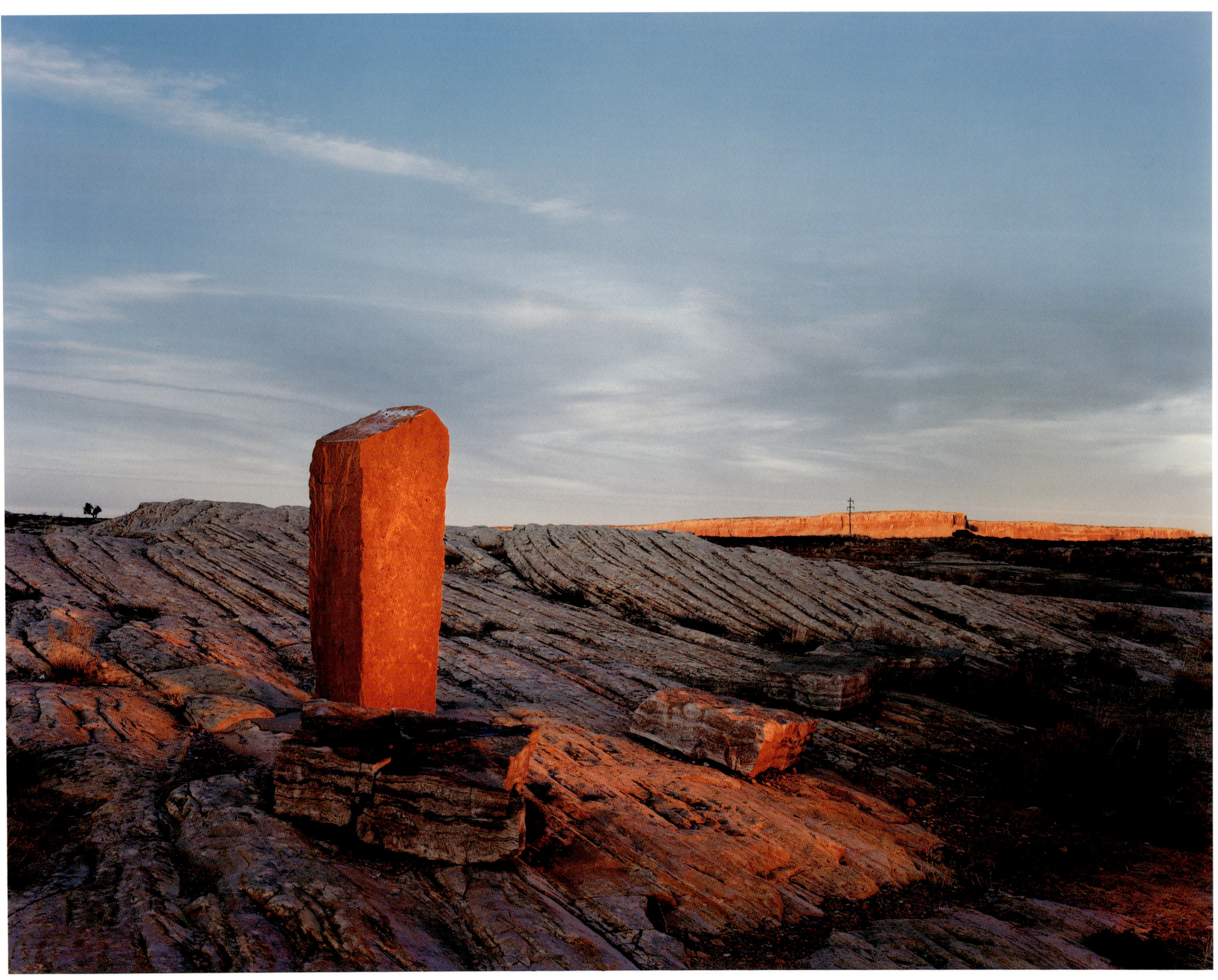

 | **Monument Commemorating Pioneer's Route,** Utah, 1997

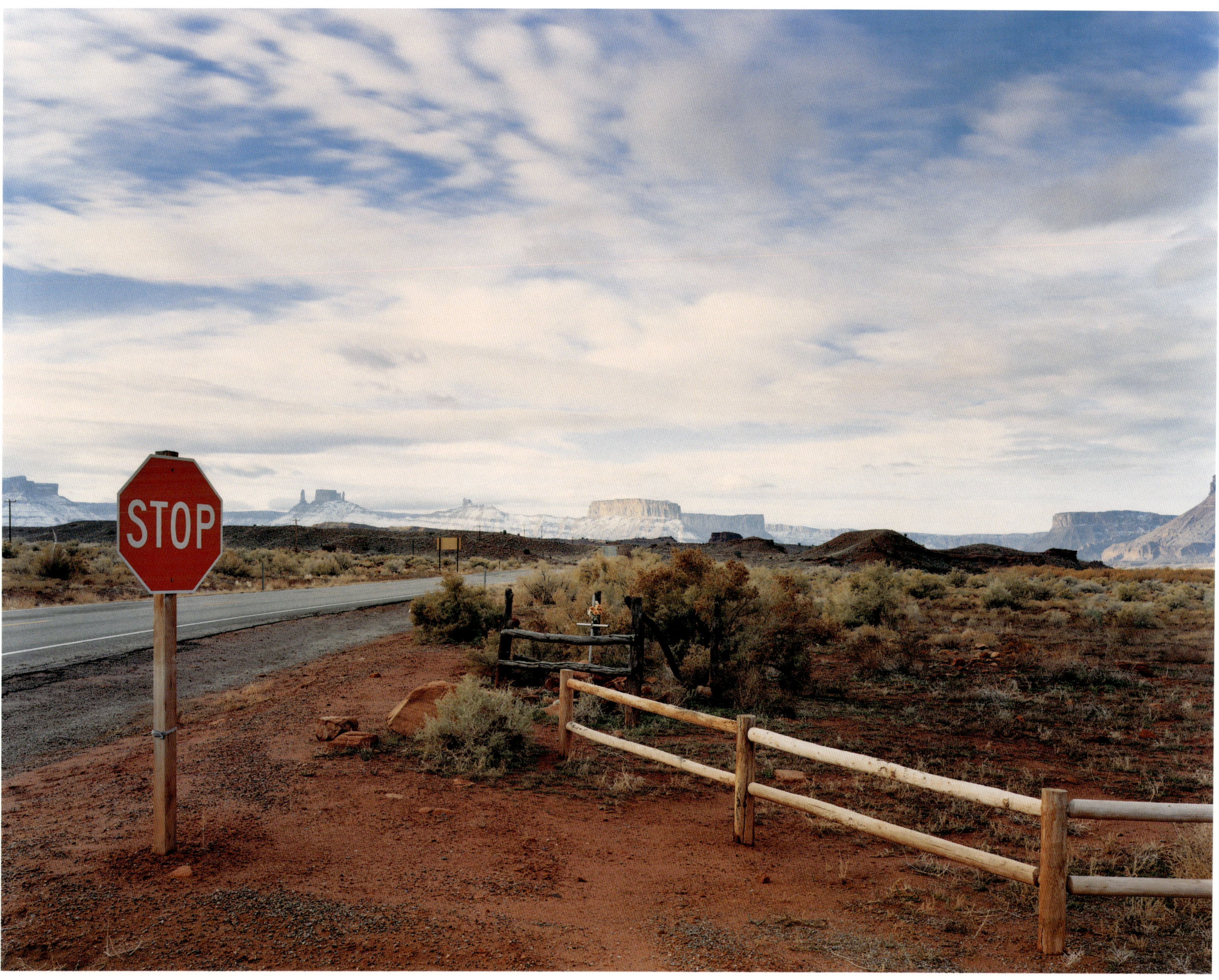

 | **Pioneer's Grave,** Utah, 1996

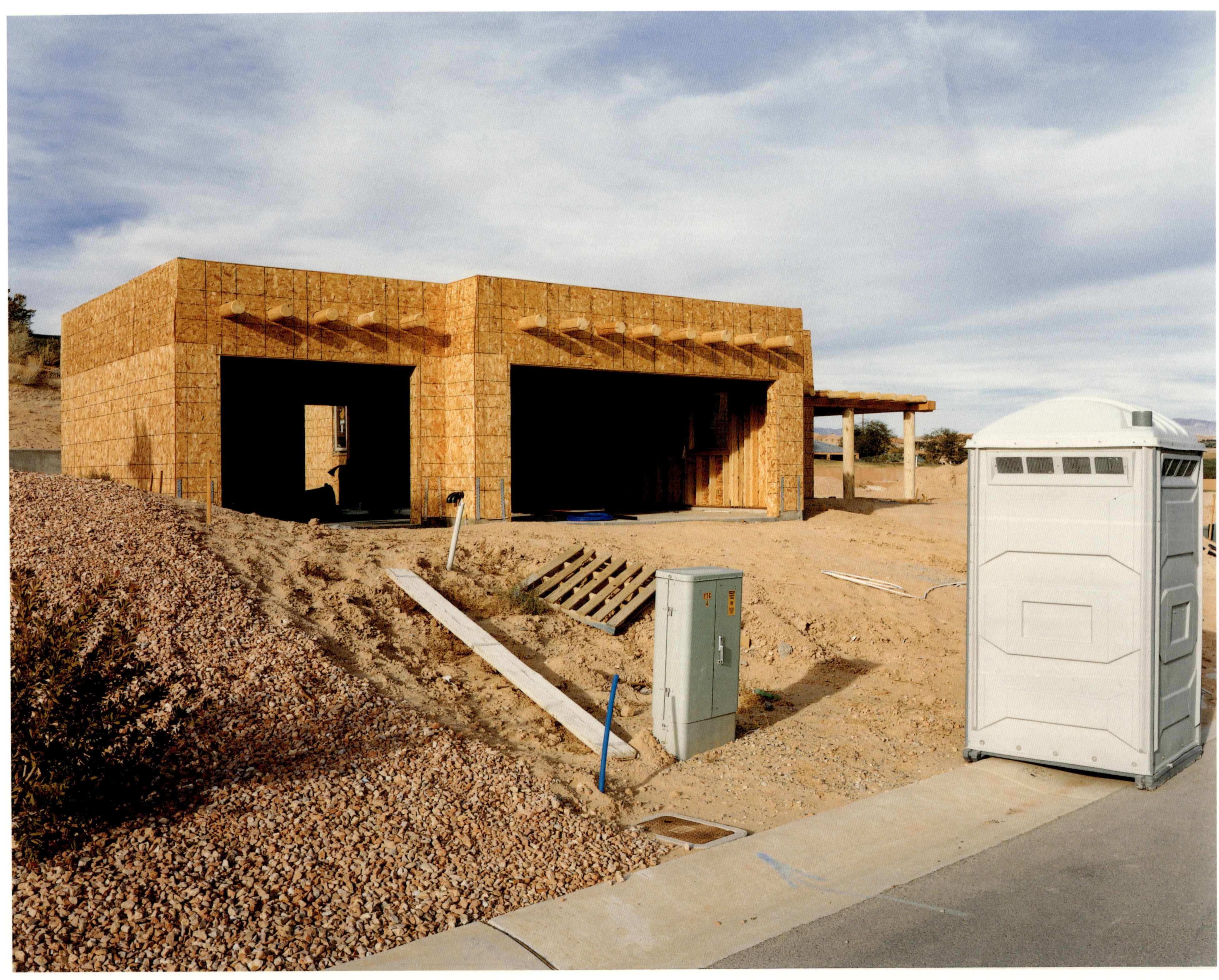

 | **Southwestern-Style House Under Construction,** Mesquite, Nevada, 2003

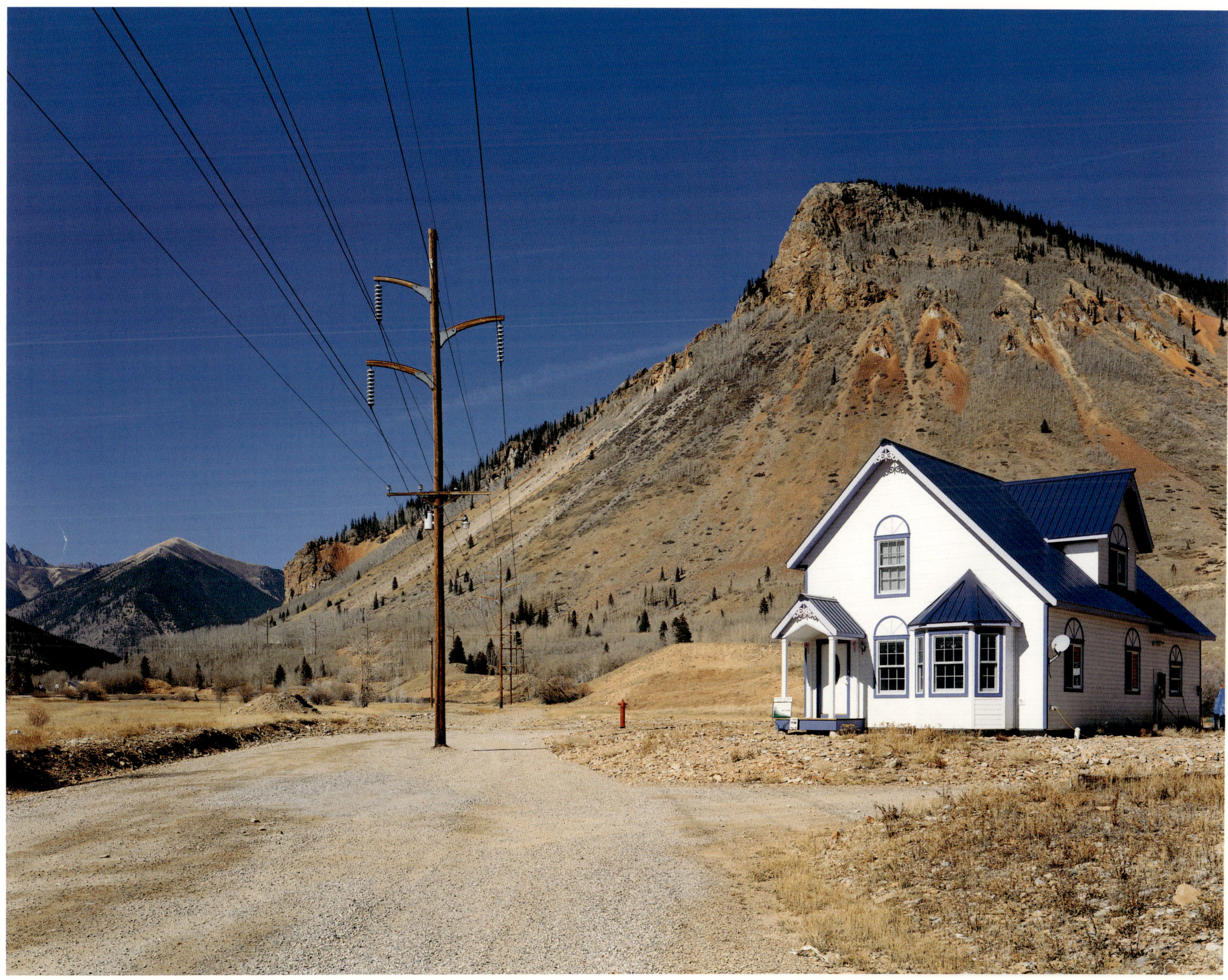

53 | **New House for Sale,** Silverton, Colorado, 2003

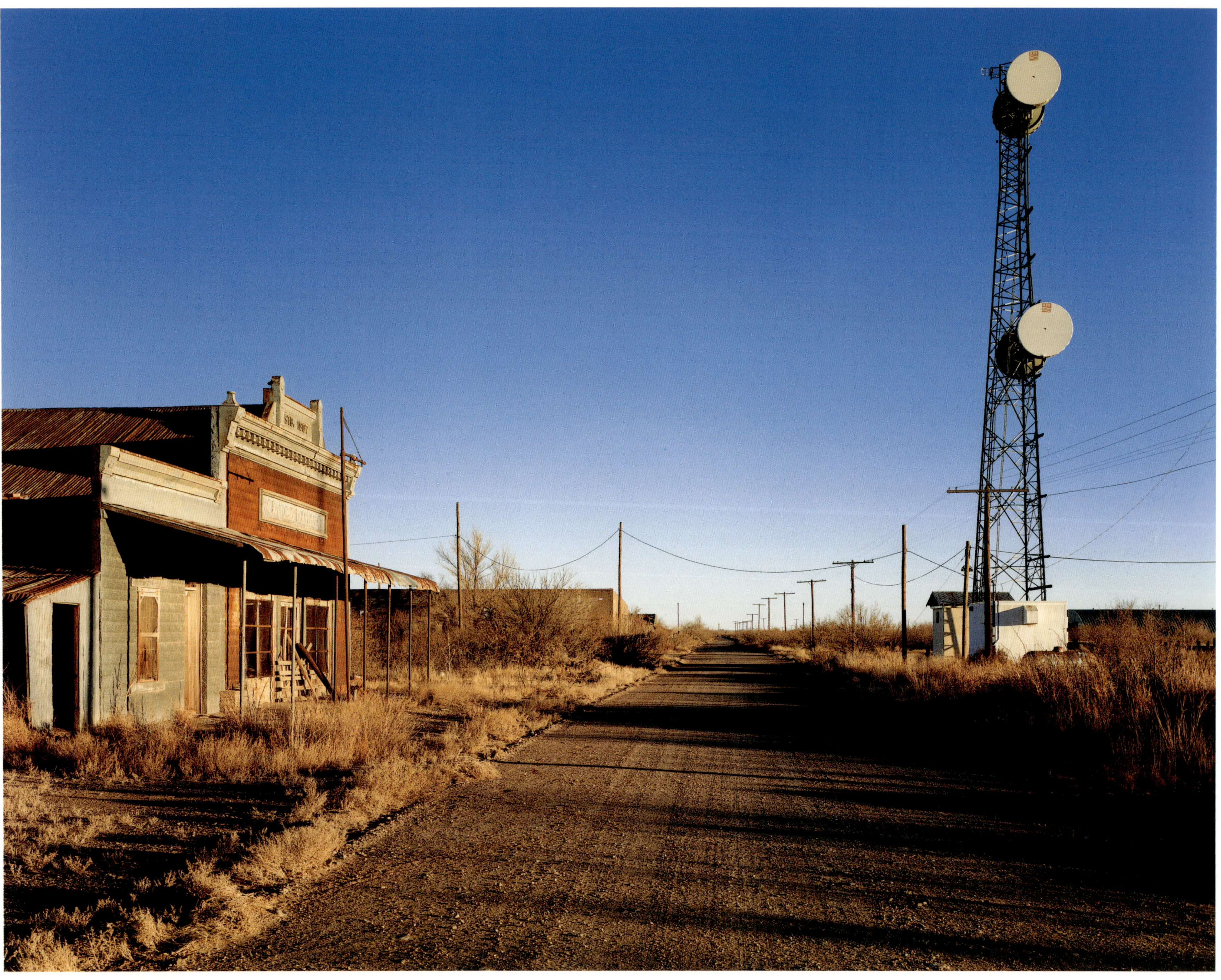

 | **Valentine, Texas,** 2001

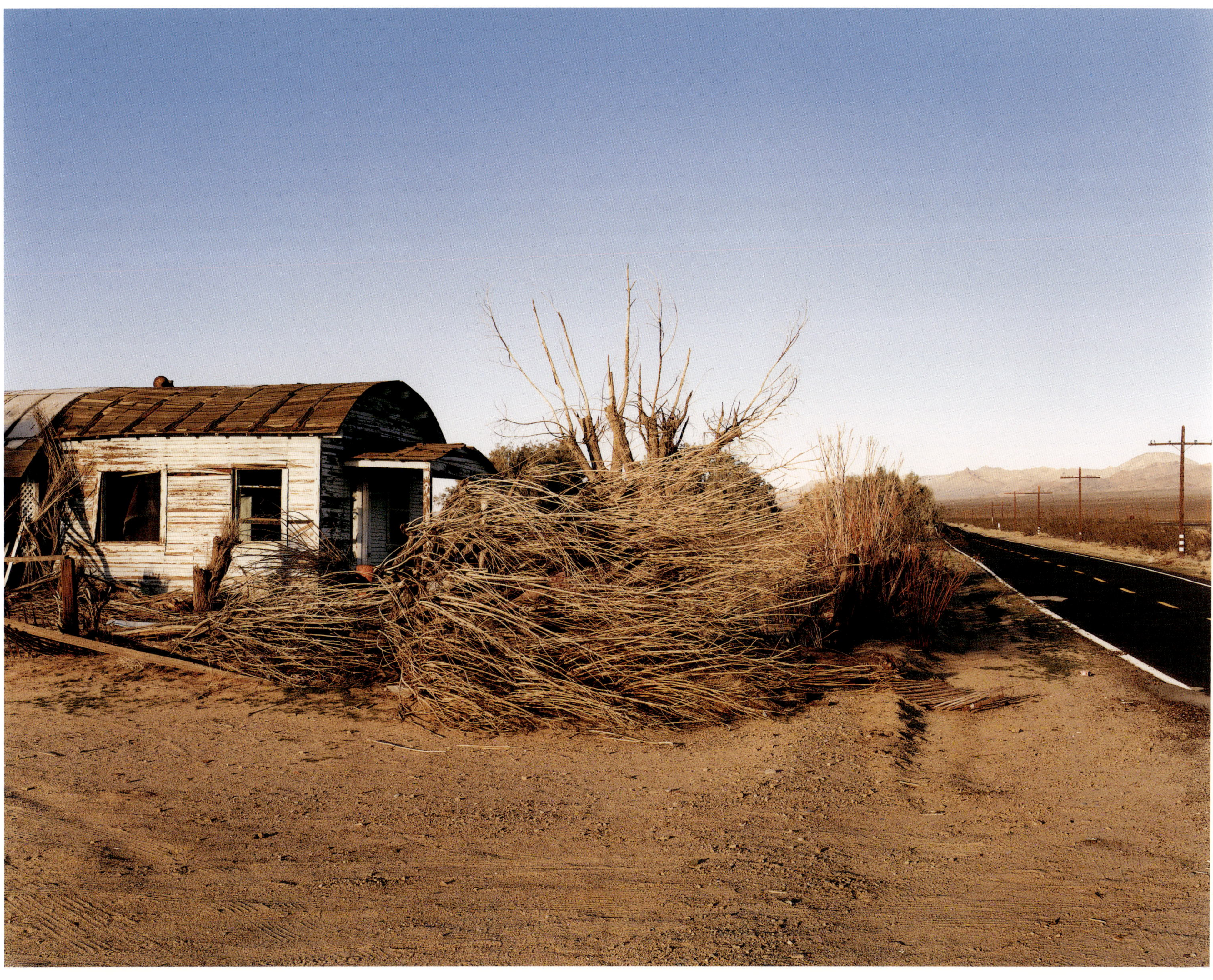

55 | Kelso, California, 2003

56 | **Wikiup, Arizona,** 2005

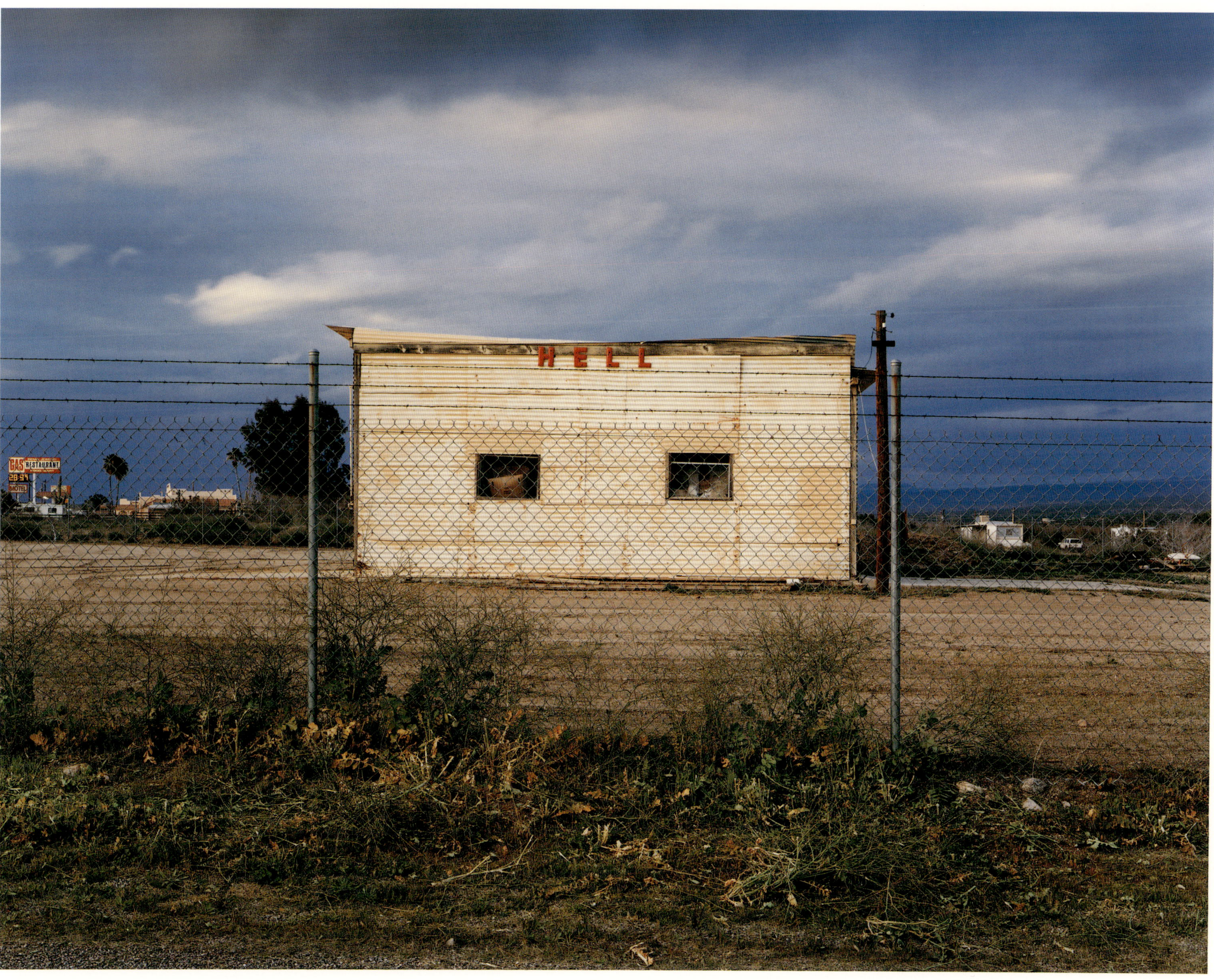
HELL
GAS
RESTAURANT
MOTEL

57 | **Broadway,** Van Horn, Texas, 2005

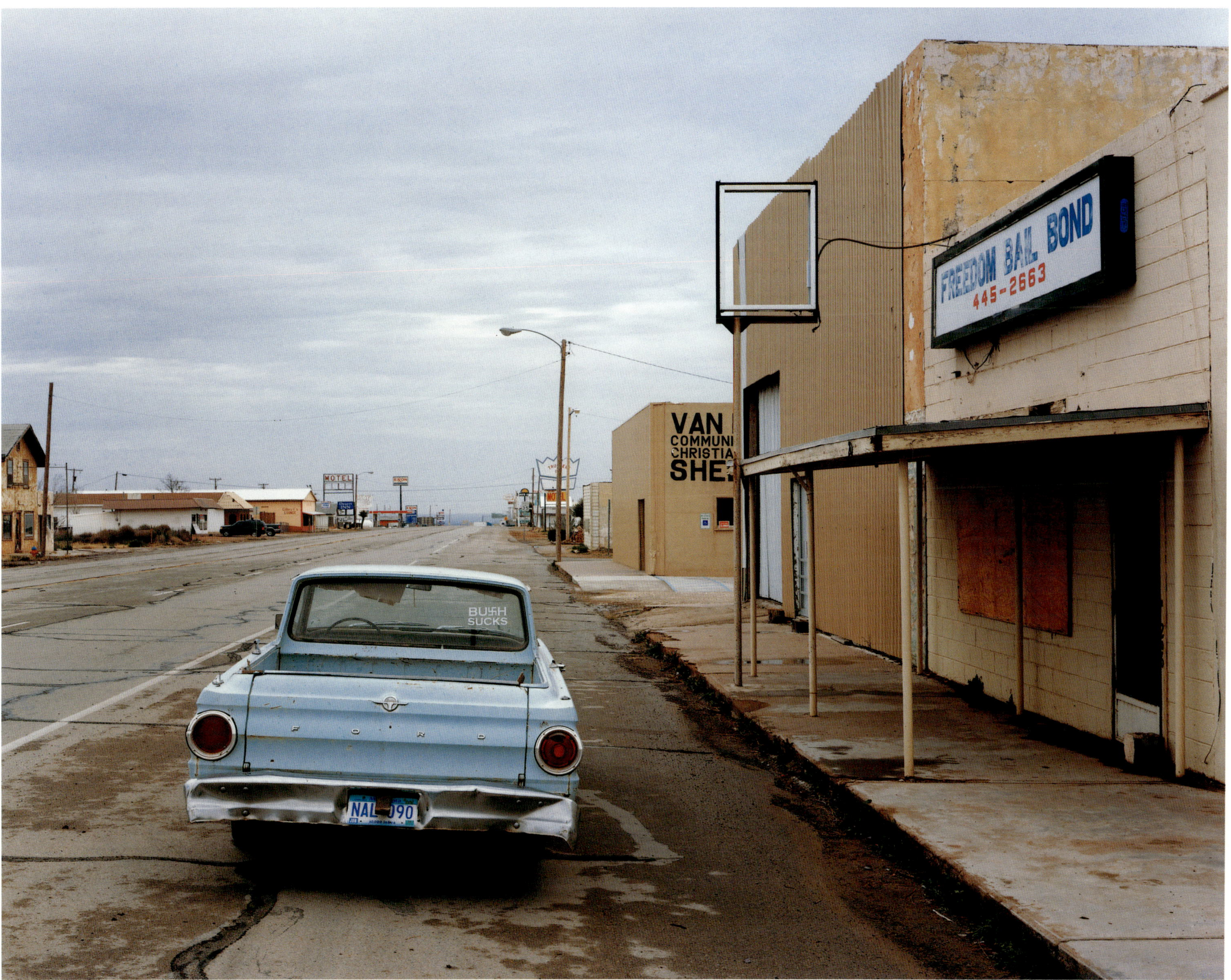
FREEDOM BAIL BOND
445-2663
VAN
MOTEL
BUSH
SUCKS
FORD

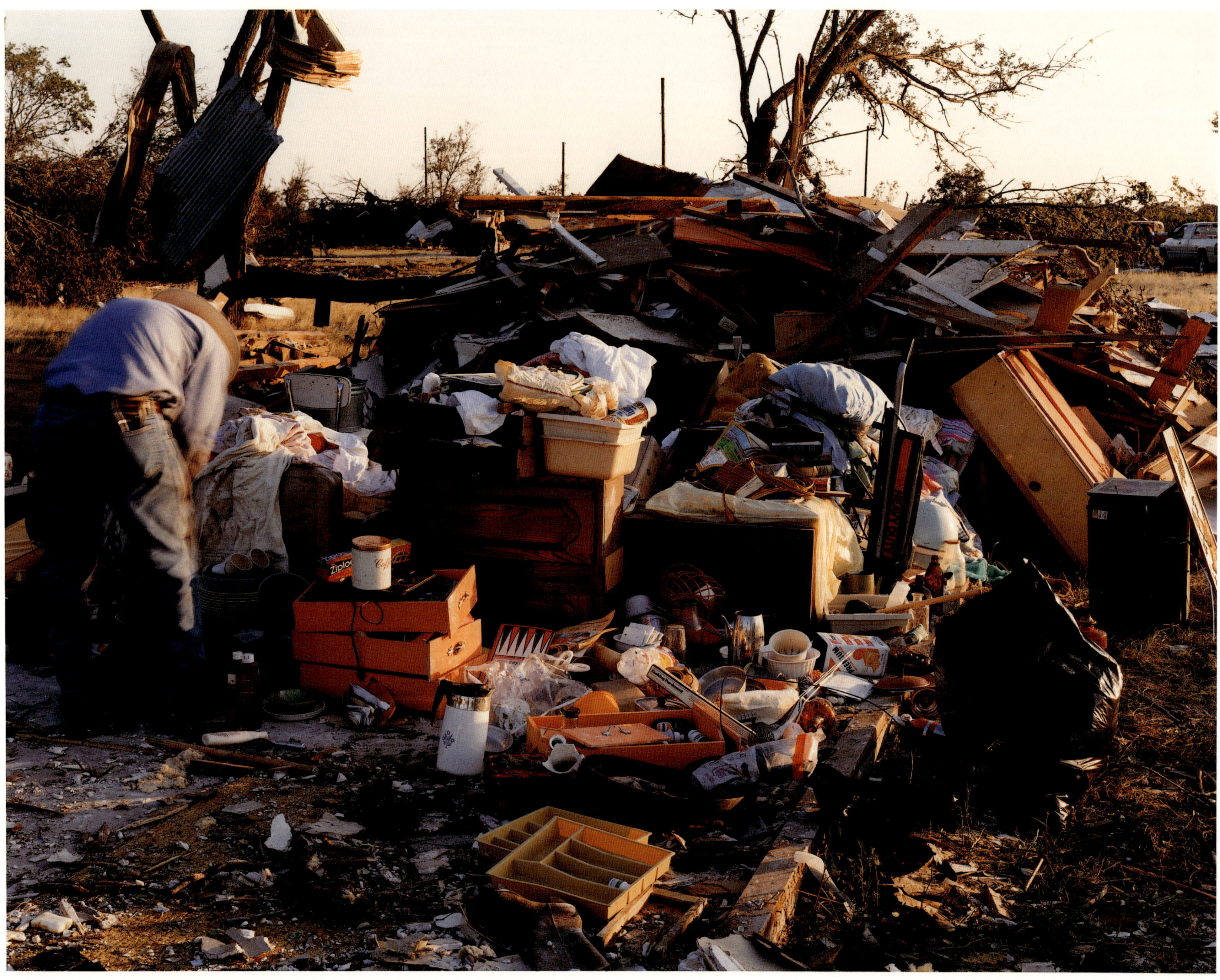

 | **Tornado Aftermath: Salvaging Usable Items,** Walling Bend, Texas, 2000

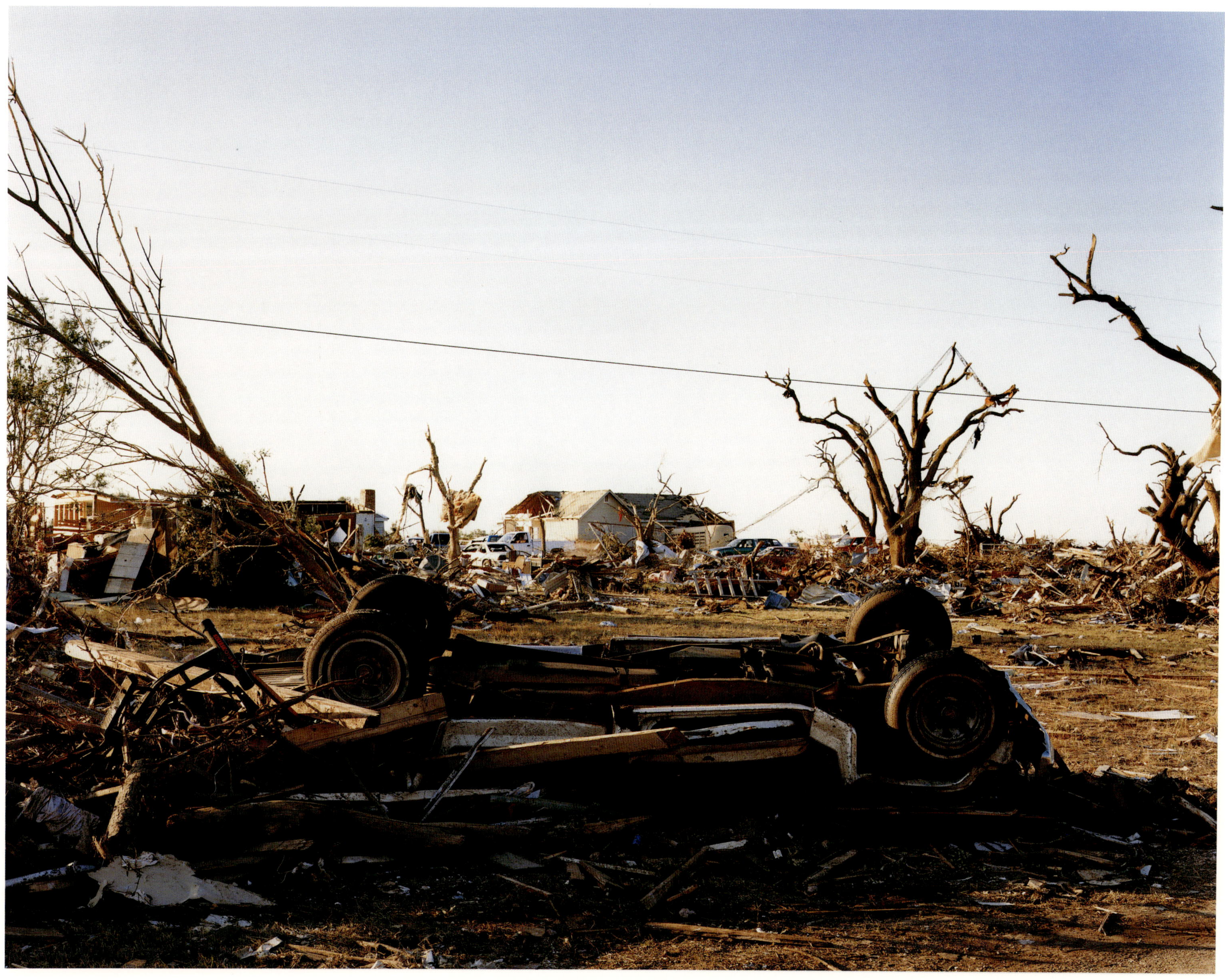

59 | **Tornado Aftermath: Flattened Truck,** Walling Bend, Texas, 2000

60 | **Homeless Man's Shopping Cart,** Bagdad, California, 2002

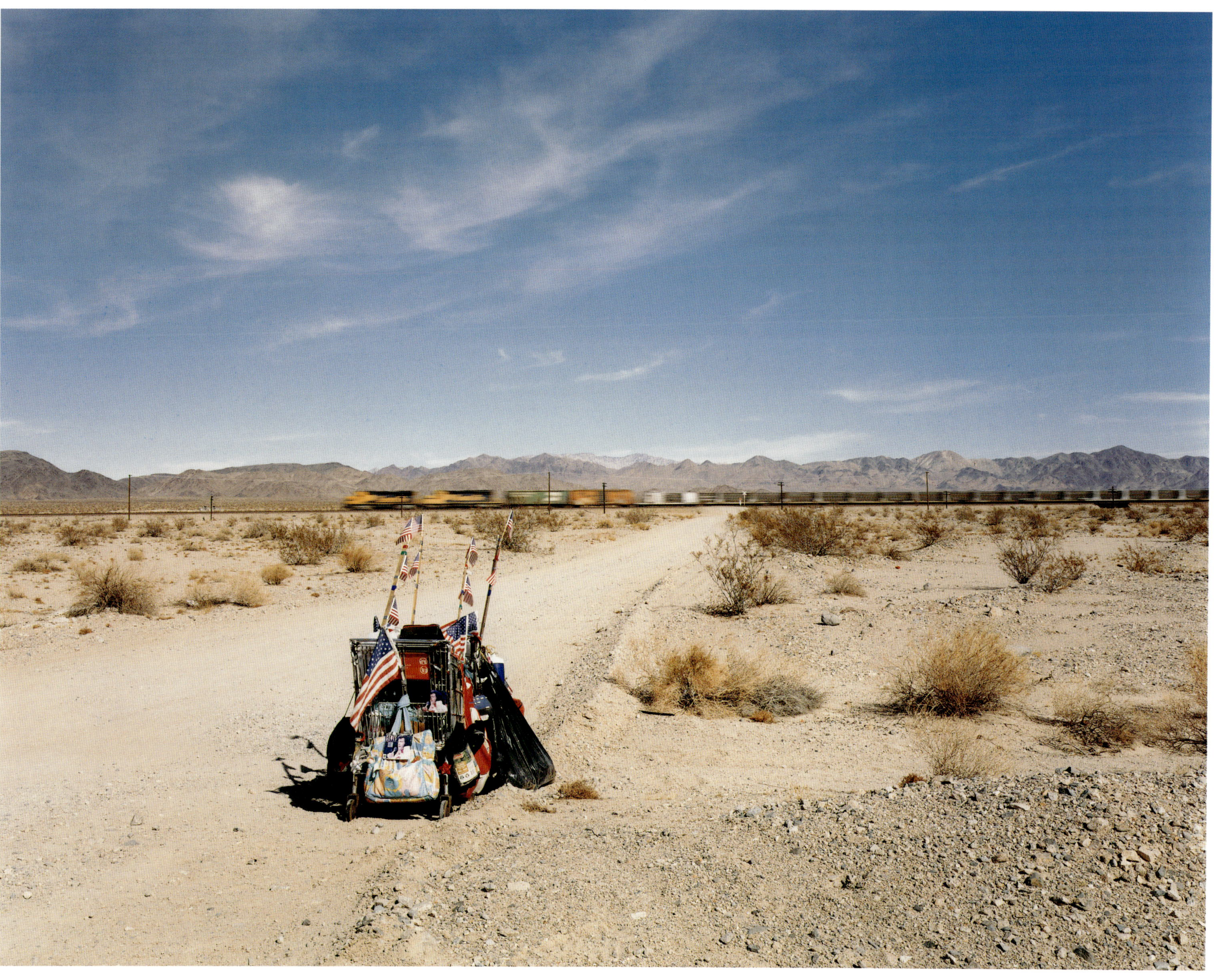

61 | **Railroad Crossing,** Mojave Desert, California, 2002

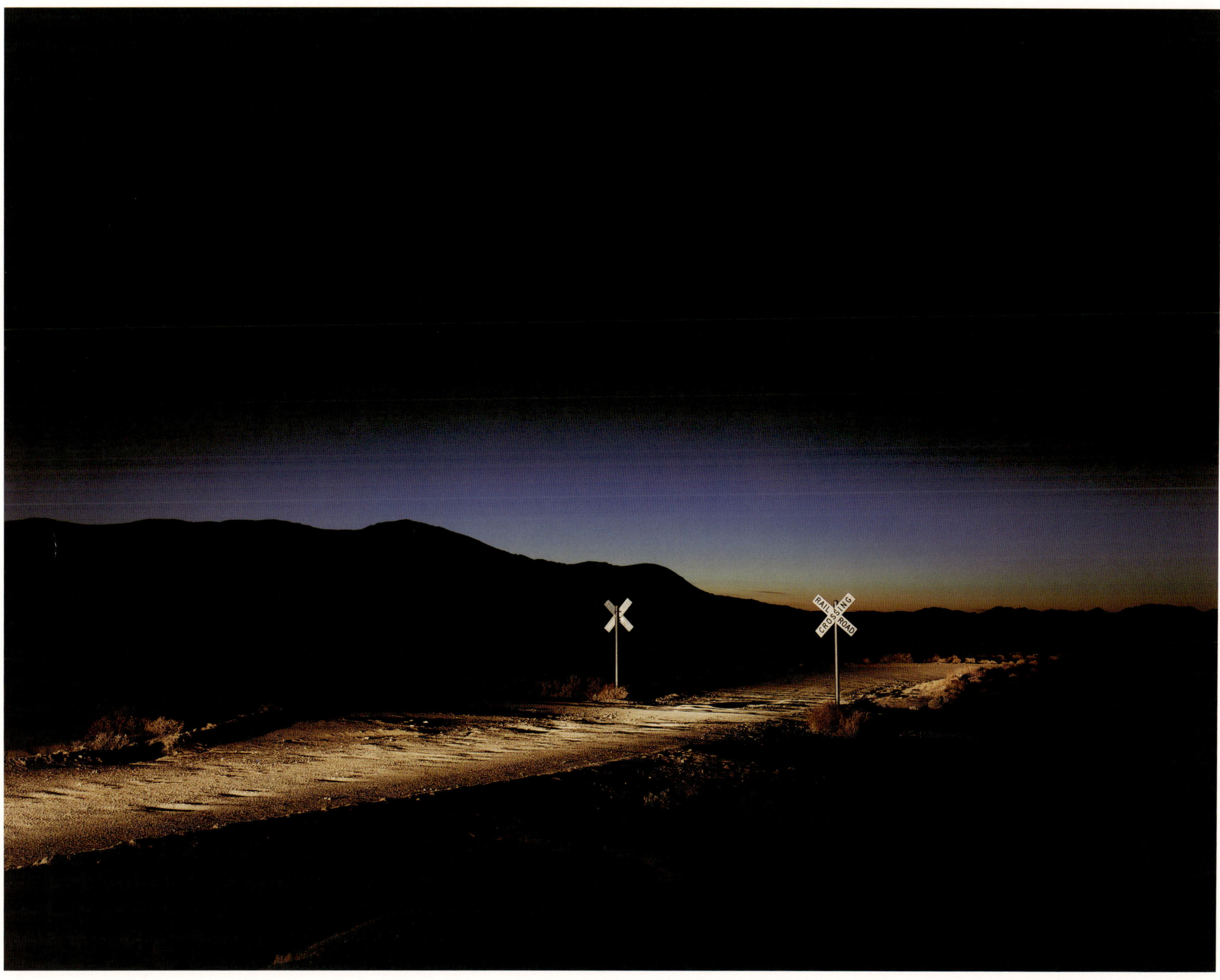
RAIL ROAD
CROSSING

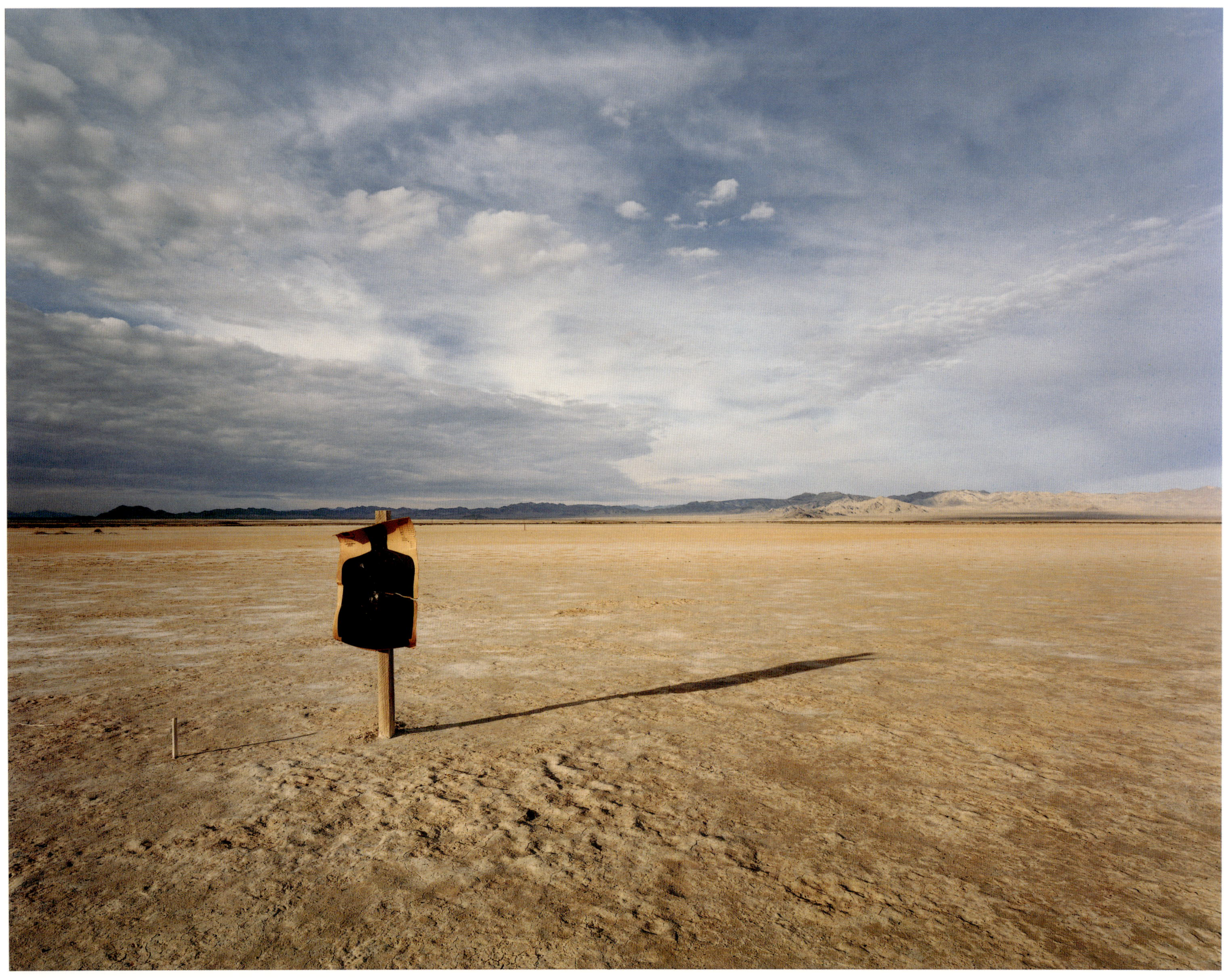

 | **Target,** Amargosa Dry Lake, Nevada, 2002

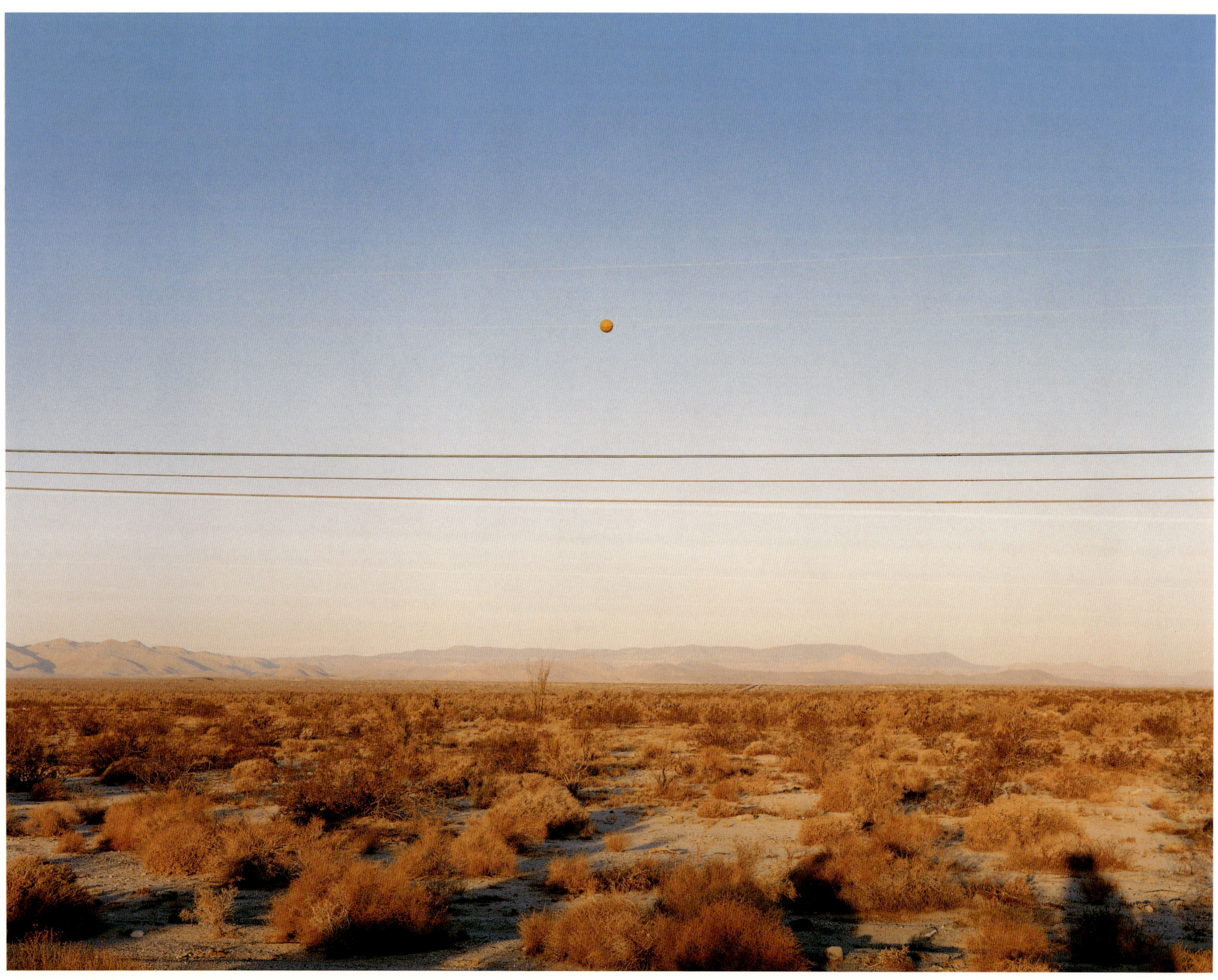

63 | **Sunrise,** Carrizo Valley, California, 1999

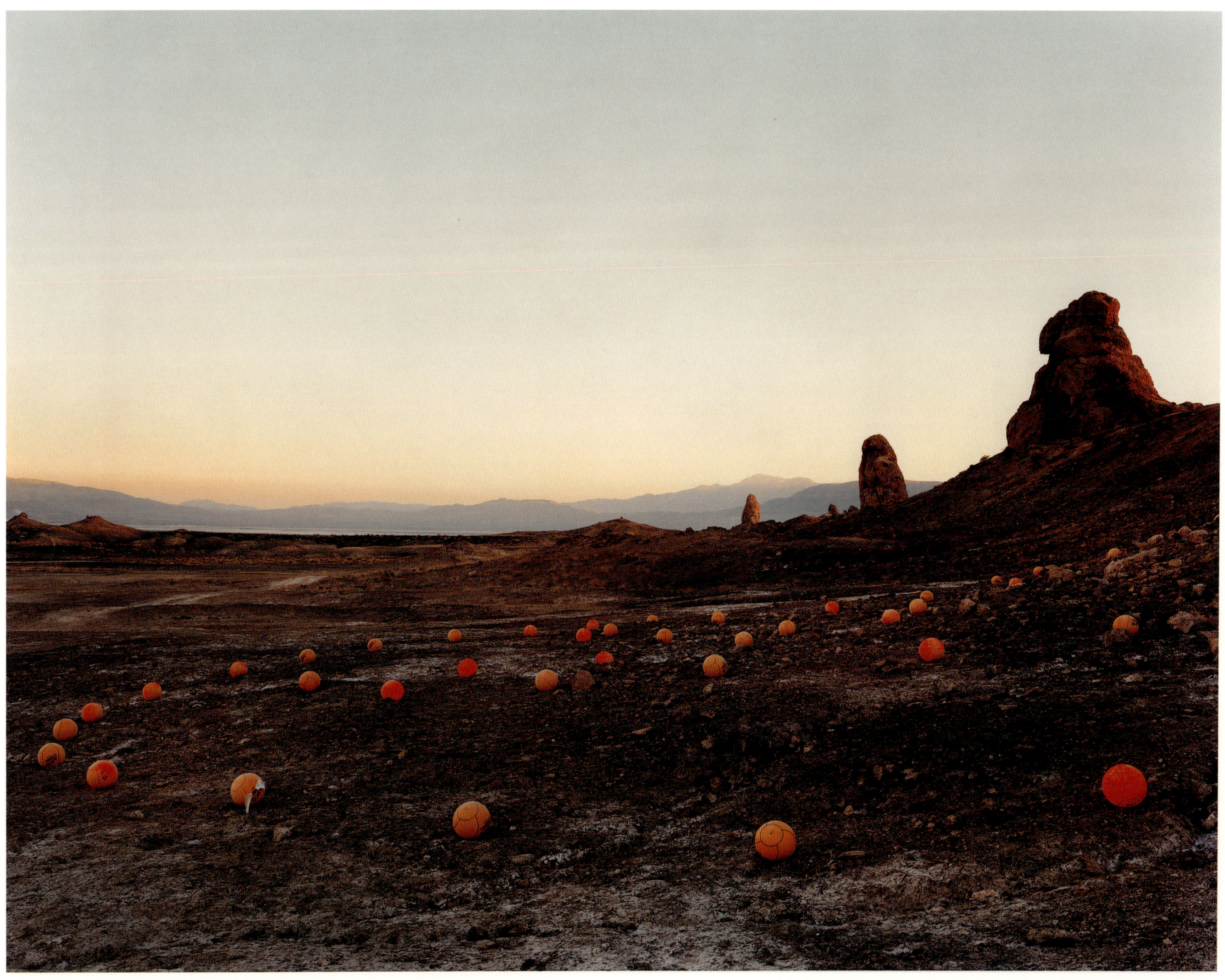

 | **Tetherballs Used by Disney Film Crew to Mark Locations for Computer-Generated Dinosaurs,** California, 1998

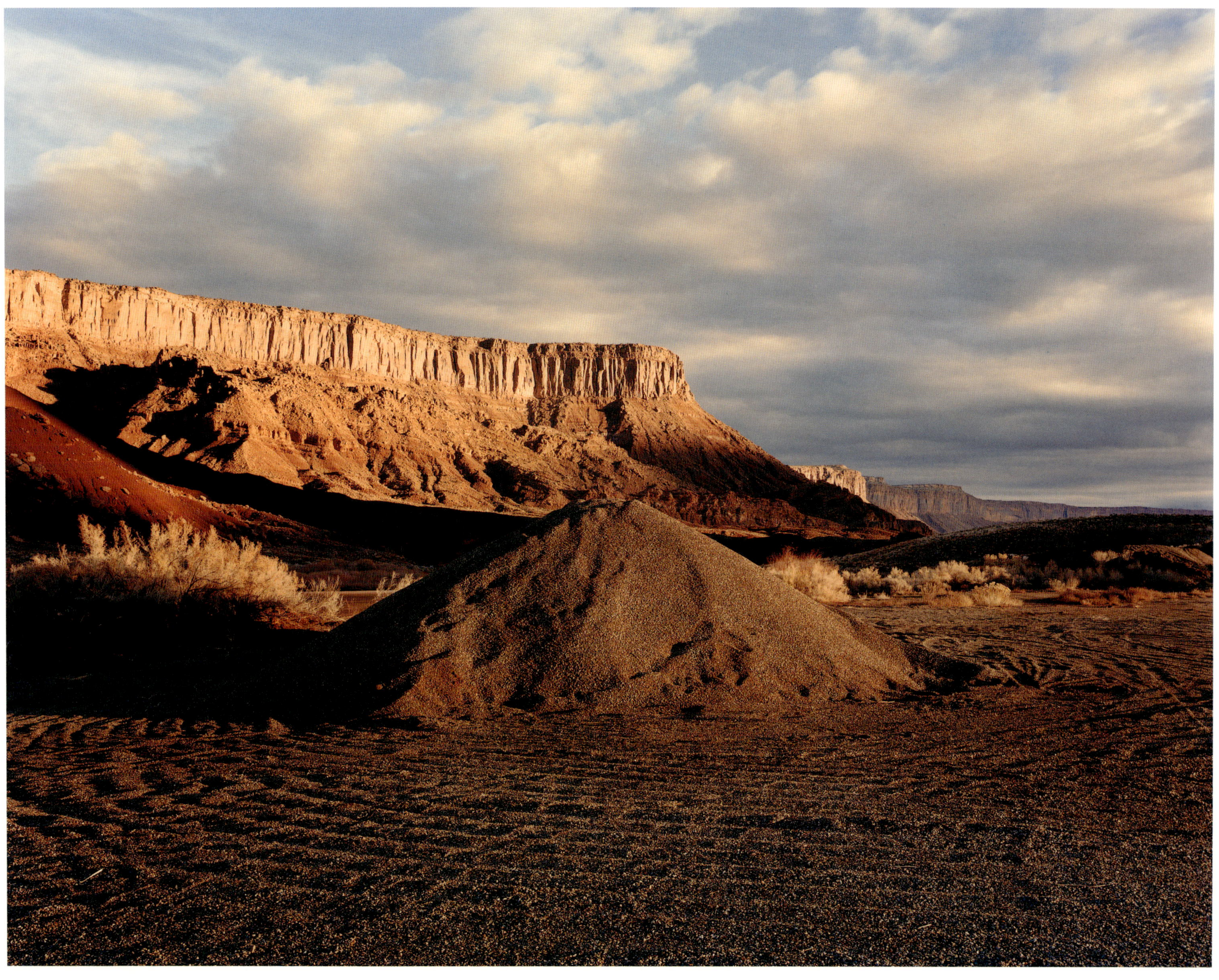

 | **Gravel Pile,** Utah, 1997

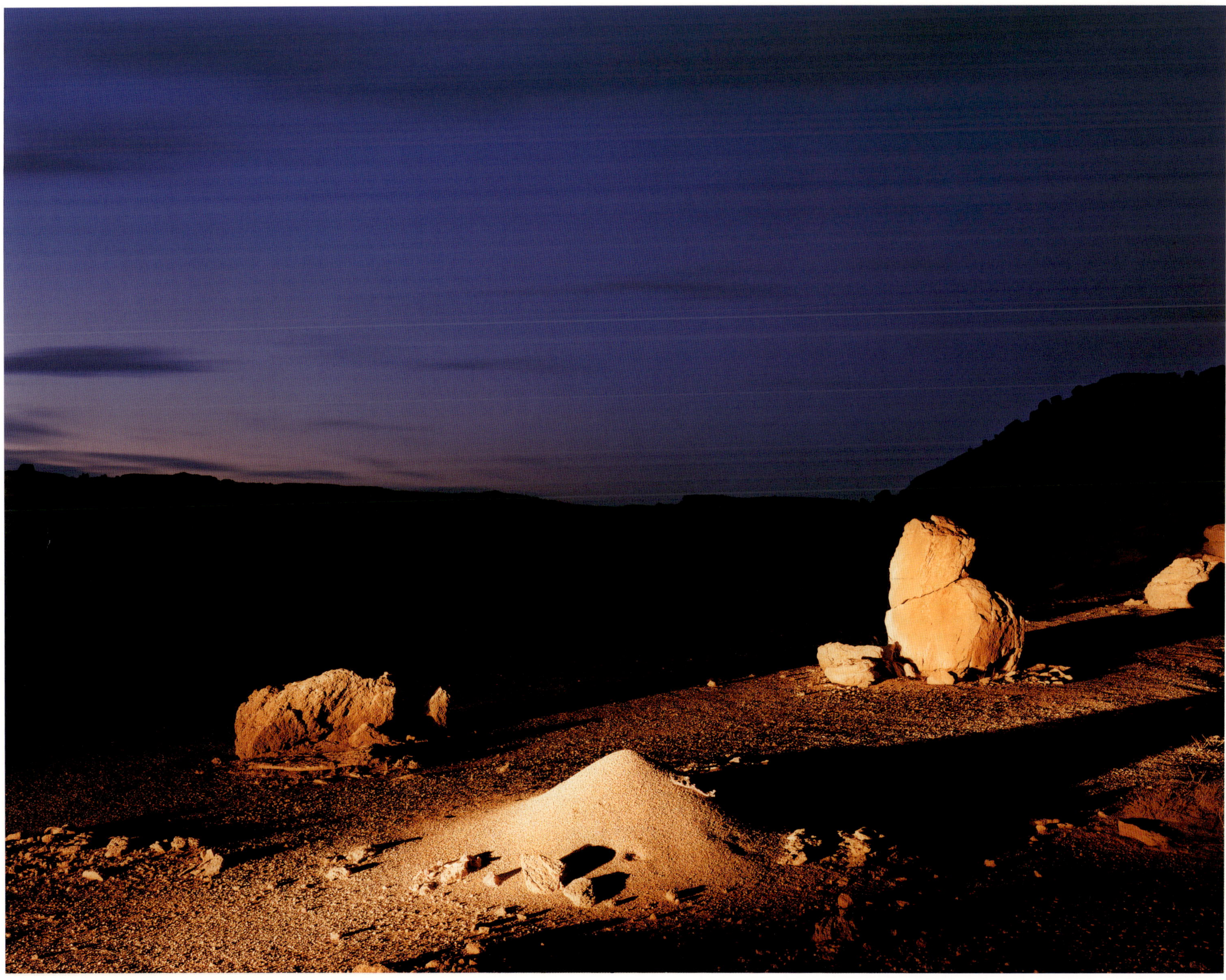

 | **Anthill,** Utah, 1996

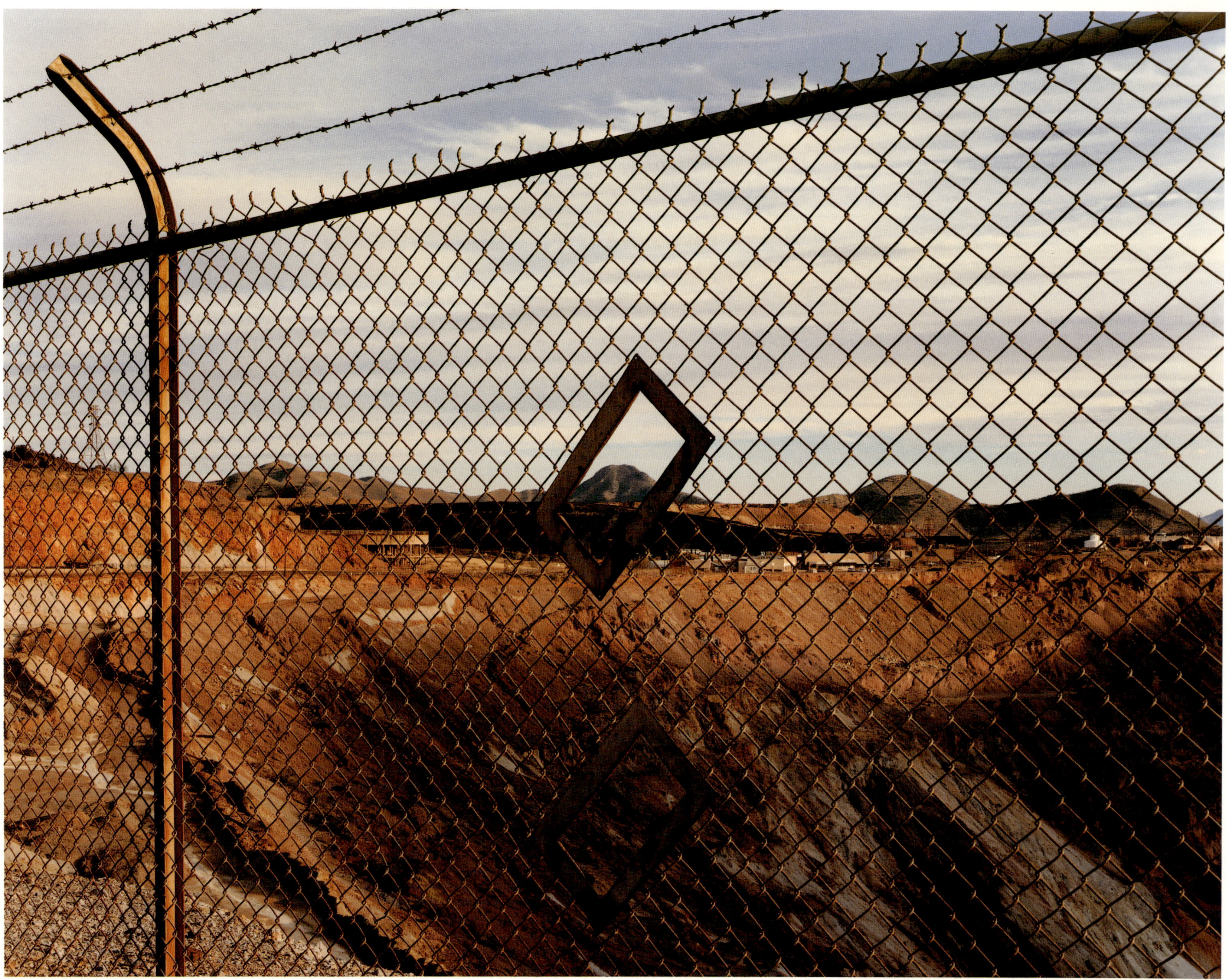

67 | **Copper Mine and Tailings Piles,** Arizona, 1998

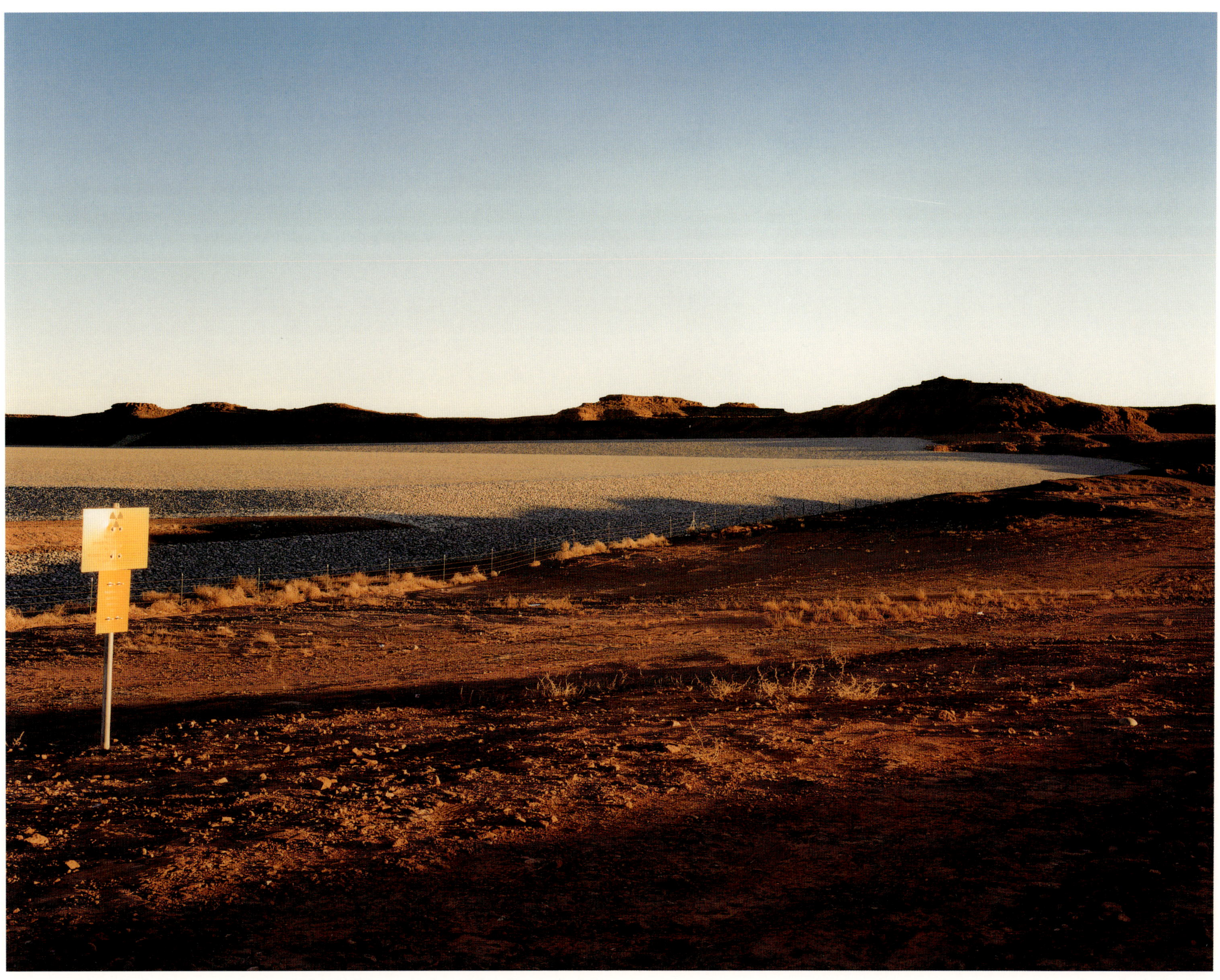

 | **Uranium Mine Tailings Disposal Site Containing 4.4 Million Tons of Radioactive Material,** Utah, 2002

69 | **Salt Trench,** Bristol Dry Lake, California, 2002

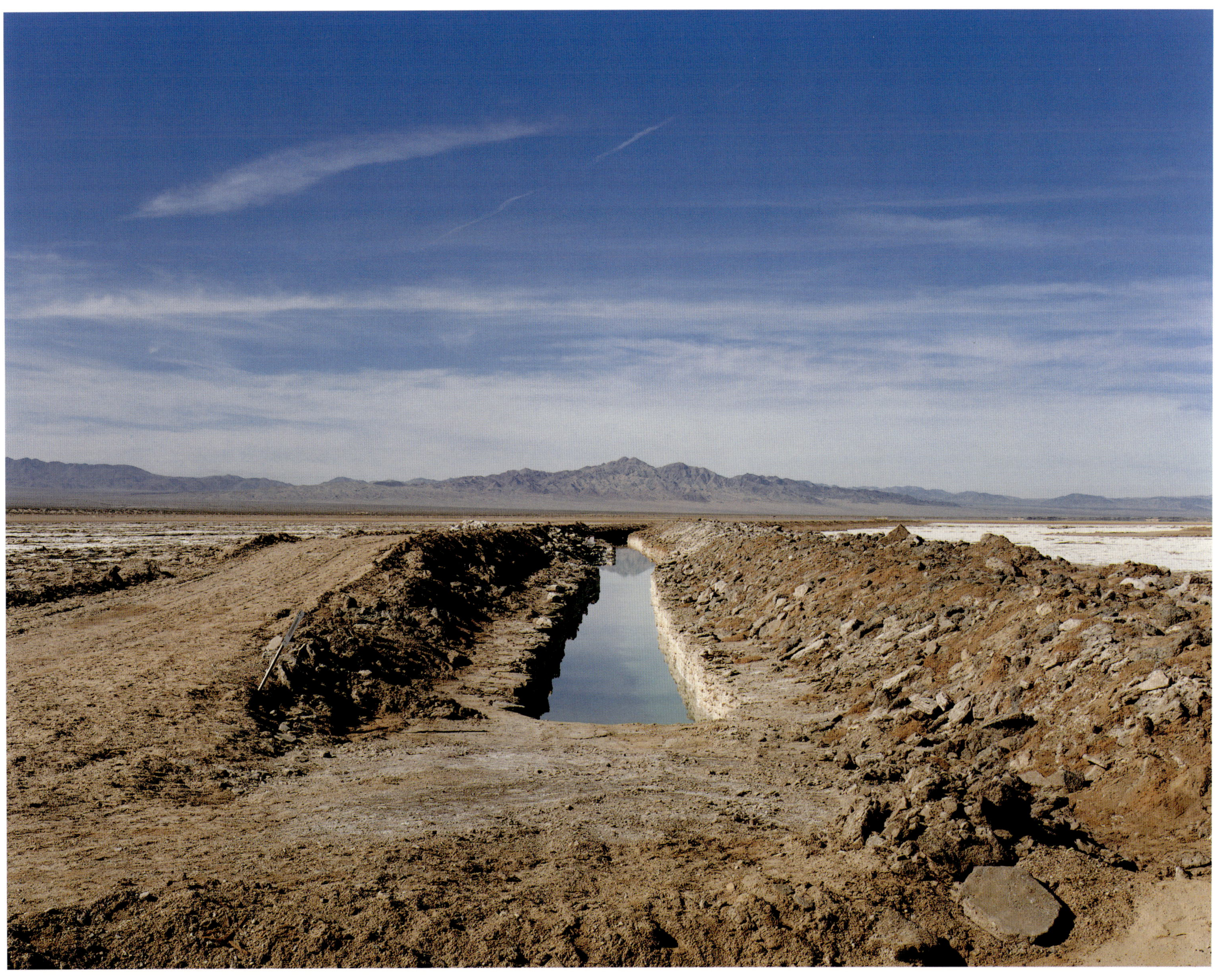

70 | **Stub End, Trona Line,** California, 2002

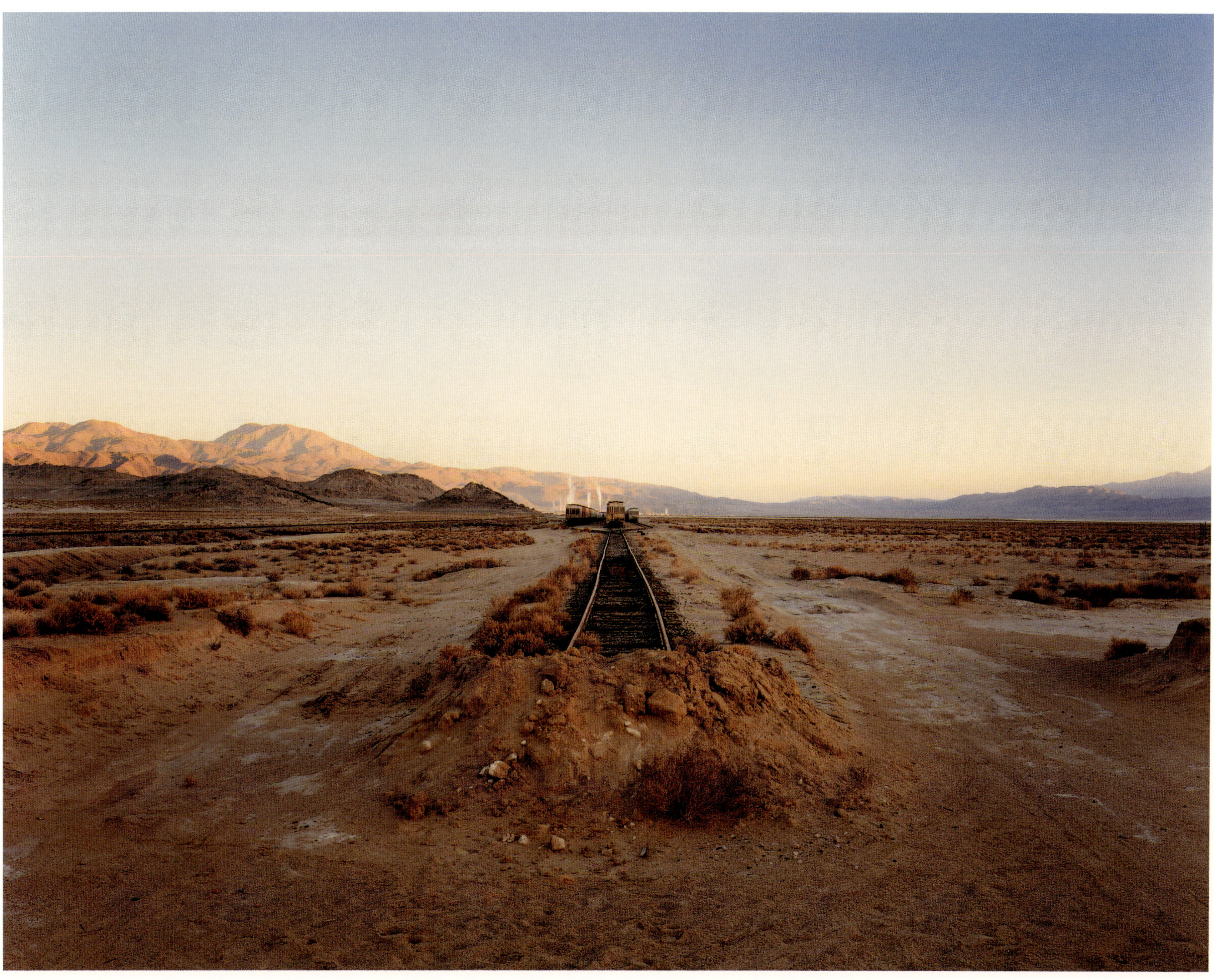

71 | **Roadside Sunset,** Northern Arizona, 1995

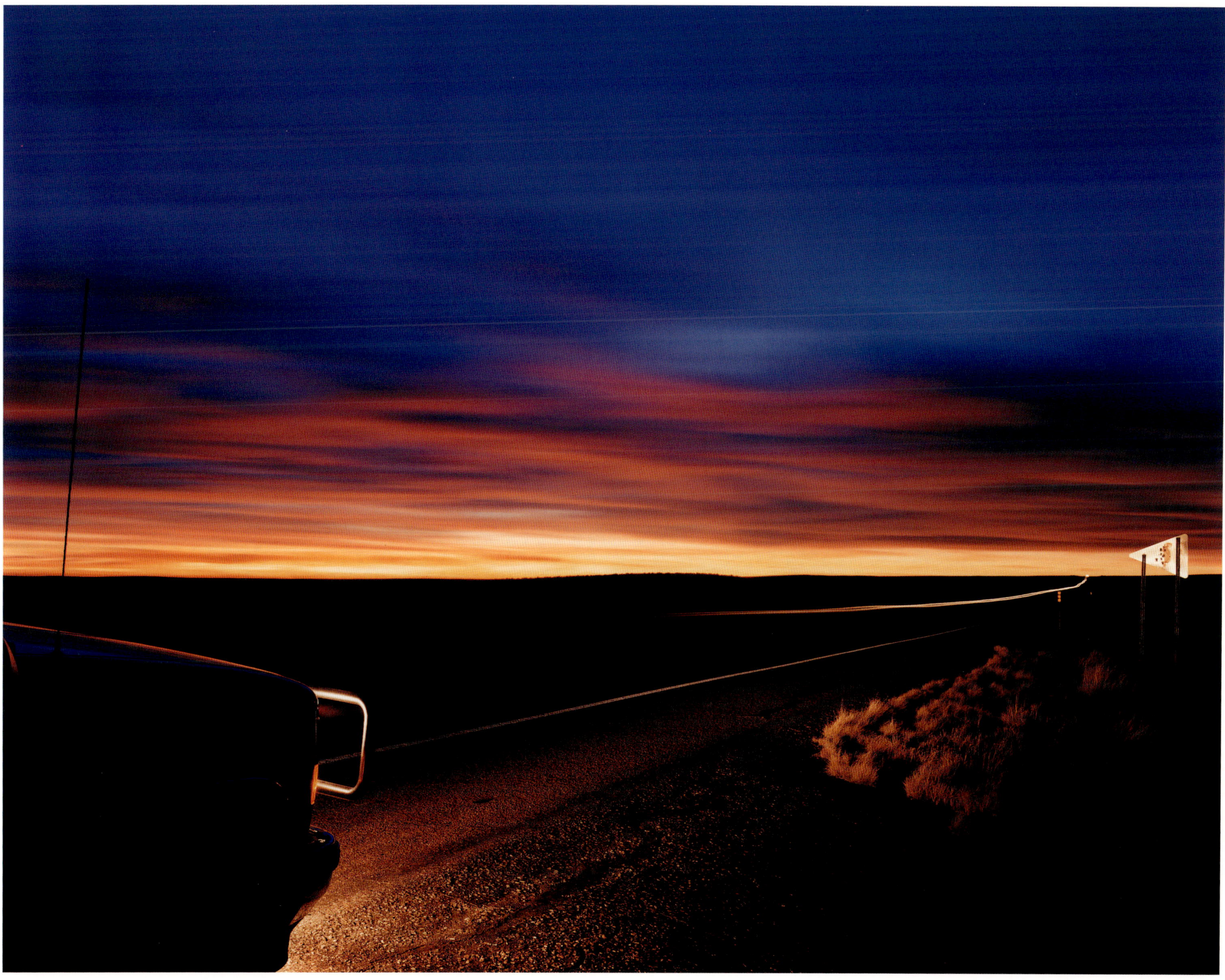

AFTERWORD

The title, *Observations in an Occupied Wilderness,* was borrowed from an essay I wrote about a dozen years ago. That thesis considered the evolution of landscape photography and my own efforts to follow suit. At the time, the deliberate oxymoron referred to the ubiquity of our imprint on and presence in the terrain. But its flexibility as a metaphor is such that I felt it could also allude to the details and paradoxes of human nature I often pursue.

The photographs in this book were made throughout the southwestern quadrant of the United States. It's a vast area, diverse in its terrain and people—both of which may demonstrate astonishingly unique attributes at times. Yet for me, notwithstanding this diversity, it has distinctness palpably apart from any other division of North America.

Were this body of work described as a portrait of the region, I would hasten to add that it would be an incomplete and idiosyncratic one, part instinctual and part conceptual. Like any artist's, my observations, occasionally rewarded or frustrated by chance, are motivated and modified by my own interests and personality. Even the purest form of documentary photography, which this work was never intended to be, presents opportunities for creation as well as transcription. Although none of the photographs in this book were manipulated or staged beyond the occasional use of artificial lighting and all were executed using entirely conventional photographic technology from negative to print—I nevertheless took advantage of the fact that what is included or excluded from the frame, and the perspective from which the camera views a scene, can be used to modify reality or suggest new meanings altogether.

ACKNOWLEDGMENTS

Publishing a book is a milestone in any artist's life. As such, it is an important time to thank those individuals who helped make it possible.

First and foremost, I am now and shall forever be grateful to my family. Everything I achieve, I owe to them. Sadly, my mother, Theresa Elizabeth Falke, passed away shortly before this went to press. It was she who introduced me to books and taught me to love and respect them. I so regret that she will not see this one in print.

This book would not exist were it not for Wendy Burton Brouws of For a Small Fee, Inc. She is my agent, my friend, and a fine photographer in her own right. She saw "it" before I did and her patience and expertise made it happen. Thank you, Agent W.

Deepest thanks to Alan Rapp of Chronicle Books for publishing this book, and for his warmth and extraordinary patience.

I am indebted to William L. Fox and Carol McCusker for their insightful and eloquent contributions to this project. My photographs are complemented by the company they're keeping.

I make my own prints, but for the tedious task of developing the thousands of eight-by-ten-inch negatives I produced over the years, I was able to rely upon the care and precision of Brian Taglang, first at Custom Process Lab, then at Lightwaves Imaging in San Francisco.

Last, but certainly not least, I have been fortunate to have friends, colleagues, and mentors who provided me with invaluable inspiration, advice, and support over the years. Among them, I am especially grateful to Ben Breard, Jeff Brouws, Diane Deming, David Donovan, Dominic Lam, Barbara McCandless, John Rohrbach, Stephen Shore, J. D. Talasek, Anne Turyn, and David Wolfe.

Thank you all.

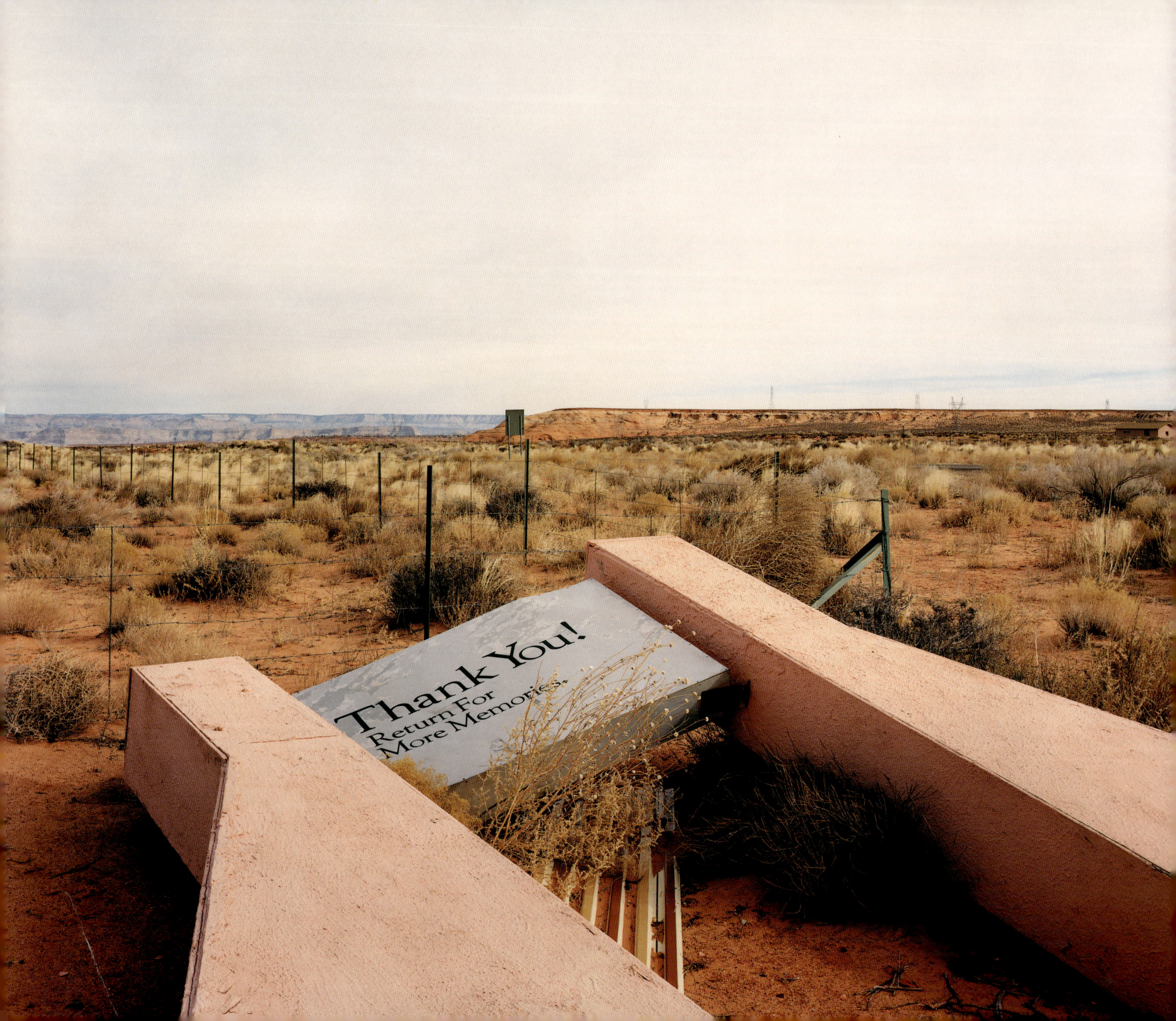
Thank You!
Return For
More Memories